inspiring
kids to
learn

The Token Economy PLAYBOOK

FIRST EDITION

BY **Denise A. Soares,** *University of Mississippi*
Walter J. Cegelka, *St. Thomas University*
AND **James S. Payne,** *University of Mississippi*

cognella®
academic publishing

Bassim Hamadeh, CEO and Publisher
Michael Simpson, Vice President of Acquisitions
Jamie Giganti, Senior Managing Editor
Miguel Macias, Graphic Designer
Jennifer Allen, Acquisitions Editor
Sean Adams, Project Editor
Luiz Ferreira, Senior Licensing Specialist
Rachel Singer, Interior Designer

First published in the United States of America in 2016 by Cognella, Inc.

Trademark Notice: Product or corporate names may be trademarks or registered trademarks, and are used only for identification and explanation without intent to infringe.

Cover image copyright © Depositphotos/nebojsa78.

Printed in the United States of America

ISBN: 978-1-63487-653-7 (pbk) / 978-1-63487-654-4 (br)

www.cognella.com   800-200-3908

Contents

Preface

This book is designed to be a one-stop shop for learning everything one needs to know to establish an effective token economy system. The authors have personally established, researched, and conducted multiple token economies with individual students, small groups of students, classrooms of students, and a three-year study with an entire school, grades 1–3.

In addition to personal experience and experimentation, the book relies heavily on three sources: *Establishing a Token Economy in the Classroom* (Stainback, Payne, Stainback, & Payne, 1973); *Living in the Classroom: The Currency-Based Token Economy* (Payne, Polloway, Kauffman, & Scranton, 1975); and a doctoral dissertation *Effect Size and Moderators of Effects for Token Economy Interventions* (Soares, 2011).

A comprehensive review of over 100 professional publications, spanning the 1950s to present day, has been reviewed and the publications referenced. Nearly all publications are abstracted and written in understandable terms to assure clarity.

Acknowledgments

Inspiring Kids to Learn: The Token Economy Playbook could not have been possible without the seminal works of Bill and Susan Stainback, Ed Polloway, Jim Kauffman, and Tom Scranton. Louise Burke, Mary Beirne-Smith, John Bittle and the late James "Smitty" Smith, Jr. and Ruth Ann Payne. They provided the teaching expertise and research skills that made each study successful and memorable. Special recognition goes to Michelle Wallace and Mary Ann Bowen for their editorial work and counsel. This book is dedicated to Barry W. Soares and Esim Erdim who ensured a finish product and to Spencer and Parker Goldson who renewed our faith in early childhood education. And finally, I would like to acknowledge my mentor, advisor, and friend, Dr. Kimberly J. Vannest. Not only has she offered her thoughts and praise, but she has given her time even when there has been very little of it to spare.

About the Authors

DENISE A. SOARES

Dr. Soares is the Assistant Chair of Teacher Education, Special Education Program Coordinator, and Assistant Professor of Special Education at the University of Mississippi. Her master's degree in Administration and Supervision was earned at the University of Houston. She earned her doctorate in educational psychology, with a concentration in special education from Texas A&M University, College Station, Texas. Prior to entering academia, Dr. Soares served as a classroom teacher and administrator for 18 years, as well as a consultant for public schools and parents. Dr. Soares serves on several state boards in Mississippi and has presented at multiple national, state, and local professional conferences. Her research focuses on applied and practical experiences in academic and behavior interventions for at-risk students, as well as examining the efficacy of those interventions in classroom settings where teachers have competing time demands.

WALTER J. CEGELKA

Dr. Cegelka is a Professor of Special Education in the College of Leadership Studies at St. Thomas University in Miami Gardens, Florida. His master's and doctoral degrees were earned at Syracuse University. Dr. Cegelka has taught and/or administered educational programs at State University of New York, the University of Northern Colorado, University of Kansas, University of Missouri, Nova Southeastern University (NSU), and Florida National College (FNC). His administrative appointments include: Assistant Director of Undergraduate Education (NSU), Campus Dean (FNC), and Department Chair (St. Thomas University).

Dr. Cegelka has written two books and numerous articles on educating exceptional children. He has directed or codirected federal and state research and training projects designed to improve the education of exceptional individuals. Dr. Cegelka has served as Education Chairman for the National Association for Retarded Children (now The Arc), a member of the Board of Directors and Associate Editor for the Council for Exceptional Children, and Consultant to the President's Committee on Mental Retardation. Dr. Cegelka has given presentations at international, national, state, and local professional conferences.

JAMES S. PAYNE

Dr. Payne is a Fulbright Scholar and presently serves as Professor of Special Education at the University of Mississippi. He served as the Dean of the School of Education from 1985 to 1996, having previously been a faculty member for 15 years at the University of Virginia. He received his doctorate, with honors, from the University of Kansas in 1970.

Dr. Payne has authored and coauthored numerous articles in professional journals and over 15 textbooks, several of which were the largest-selling texts in their respective areas. *Mental Retardation: Introduction and Personal Perspectives* was the largest-selling introductory text in the area of mental retardation for over 14 years. *Strategies for Teaching the Mentally Retarded* was the largest selling methods text in the area of mental retardation for 12 years. *Exceptional Children in Focus* was the biggest-selling supplementary text in Special Education for 12 years. In 1990, Dr. Payne turned the authorship of the three texts over to students and colleagues so he could focus on his writing, mainly on business and industry, for the general public. The three texts continue to sell well and all are in their 9th and 10th editions. He has consulted with large and small organizations and has been a regular consultant with the Senior Executive Institute, teaching city managers team building and strategic planning, and the Federal Executive Institute, teaching federal executives vision building and motivation.

CHAPTER 1

Is and Isn't

Secretary of Education Arne Duncan acknowledged recently that classroom management has become a huge issue that impedes learning. A teacher cannot teach a classroom if he or she can't manage the classroom environment. The following story is an example:

Morning is the most chaotic part of the day for a teacher. You may have a bit of prep time, but almost immediately after arriving at work, you're likely to be greeting children and trying to welcome them to school in a way that makes them excited to be there. Amid rushed exchanges with parents on their way to work, you might be entrusted with notes on how that child's morning is going ("Today's gonna be a rough one"), someone is leaving early for a doctor's appointment, or someone's sister was ill last night so they should be watched for signs of not feeling well. These are just a few examples of the information you're expected to keep in your brain about a child.

Now that the children have arrived and are seated nicely at their desks, the scene can be described:

> *Mrs. Marco, the teacher, is at the front of the classroom, sitting at her desk with her hands folded, staring into space and dreaming of a career change and ignoring the disruptions in the classroom. This is what Mrs. Marco sees: Hailey is at the pencil sharpener, constantly sharpening her pencil, while Hannah is whispering and passing notes to Jennifer, who is giggling and making faces at Hannah. Jason is in the back of the room, carving artwork into his desk. Bryce announces loudly that he "forgot to bring my pencil" (or pen or notebook), so therefore he cannot work today. Kade is in the back, playing imaginary soldiers and pretending to "shoot" his classmates. Sydney daydreams while brushing her hair. Megan pretends to work. Justin plays drums with his pencil and pen. Tim is mumbling and ripping paper out of a notebook, crumbling it. Jamie reads a comic book and Jennifer is sleeping. Tina jabs Jennifer to get her to wake up. Someone in the group whistles the latest pop song. Sebastian yawns and stretches his arms out to hit Bella, who is throwing small objects across the room. Mrs. Marco is unfazed by the seemingly chaotic classroom.*

Discipline is an interesting riddle. Your patience is tried, as students don't listen; yet if you lose your cool, the kids won't respect you. Plus, you'll lose your voice.

Without question, viable communication is essential to the educational process. Very few educators would dispute that fact. We believe a token economy provides a clear and precise system of communication. An analogy can be drawn between a token economy and the monetary reward system, which operates primarily in adult life in this country. Just as almost every adult understands the meaning of money, nearly every child who participates in a classroom token economy can understand the meaning of tokens. We think this system can enhance teacher-student communication and lead to both superior performance and personal growth.

This book will explain how to establish a token system in detail. After studying the book, the teacher will have sufficient information to develop and successfully execute a token system. The authors reviewed most, if not all, published materials pertaining to token systems and implemented several successful token systems. We concluded that a token system could be used as an effective educational tool with most children. Our conclusion led to the development of *Inspiring Kids to Learn: The Token Economy Playbook.*

We believe every teacher, whether in elementary, secondary, or special education, should at least be exposed to the benefits a token system can effect for certain students. Every teacher-training institution should provide at least enough information pertaining to token systems to enable a professionally trained person to discuss the problems and values of such a system intelligently and hopefully provide an opportunity to actually participate in such a system.

A token system is not a cure-all. A token system in a classroom will not *make* kids learn; it will not make children smarter. It might help the students settle down so that the teacher can get their attention; it might even stimulate students to want to learn certain academic concepts. It certainly will help teachers communicate with children. It cannot produce miracles, in spite of what some behavioral specialists claim.

The purpose of any educational endeavor is to effect change in the learner in some way. The child exposed to a first grade teacher should be different at the end of first grade than she was at the beginning. Teachers want to see educational success and growth in children. The worst would be for a teacher to teach all year using his educational strategies and skills only for a child to remain unaffected.

Most certainly, we must employ teachers who wish to help children, but we must also terminate teachers who are unable to get kids interested in learning. A teacher who uses a token system is using a powerful tool, and he most certainly may use this tool to do harm as well as good. The teacher must consider the welfare of children at all times. No child can participate in a well-executed token system and remain unchallenged and unchanged.

This book is about a powerful system that will enable teachers to be effective, but its positive or negative results lie directly in the hands of the teacher. This system is not easy to implement; it is time consuming and requires hard work. If used imprecisely, it could cause chaos in a matter of seconds. We educators have structured classrooms where children are educationally dying. We have permissive schools where children are committing educational suicide. What we must develop is a classroom that will accommodate *individuals* and allow these individuals to function at their own rates on their own levels. The model classroom must have a teacher who can reach all children and get each one excited about learning, providing exciting, well-planned activities, ideas, and content, accompanied by effective methods of teaching. We must not pump up a dull curriculum with any teaching technique; most certainly, we don't want to pump up a dull curriculum with tokens. This book won't tell you what content to teach; but it will give you a powerful way to teach that gets results.

Before proceeding to the specifics of what a token system is and how to develop and implement one, we would like to clarify a couple of points:

1. Some teachers remark that they have tried a token system and it didn't work. Later, we find their idea of a system was handing out a token a week, or at best, a token a day for good behavior or for completing an arithmetic assignment. To be perfectly clear, if the teacher has not given out *at least* 25 tokens per child per day, he hasn't used a system. In order

for the token system to work, the teacher must communicate—and communicate often. The same is true with praise. Some teachers say children don't respond to praise; but in observing their classes, one finds their rate of praise is quite low. Upon bringing this to their attention, they may respond with "I didn't have time," or "They didn't do anything worth praising." In order to test whether tokens (or praises) work, they first have to be *given out, disseminated, and dispensed.*

2. Sometimes, token systems fail because the tokens can't be exchanged for anything the child wants or is worth getting. Earned tokens must be exchanged for something desired.

CASE STUDY

First-year teacher Ms. Williams struggles to teach content to her fourth-graders for more than ten minutes without addressing inappropriate behavior. She remembers learning a "guaranteed technique" and sets out to implement a token economy. After a run to a teachers' supply store (too expensive) and a local discount mart (nothing appropriate), she purchases some supplies and spends most of the weekend designing her own system. Since her classroom theme is bees (who can fly, even though physics tells us they can't), she creates token earning cards with her theme "You're Buzz'n" and laminates them. Fifty bucks and a trip to a dollar store yield some tangible backup reinforcers such as pencils, stickers, small bottles of bubbles, and cheap headphones. She then posts her rules:

1. Raise your hand to speak
2. Work quietly
3. Keep hands to self
4. Use soft and sweet voices
5. Keep our classroom neat.

"You're Buzz'n" token cards created, backup reinforcers purchased, and rules posted, Ms. Williams is ready.

School starts Monday morning, and Ms. Williams explains her system to the students, but by Wednesday, she is no longer consistently passing out "You're Buzz'n" cards and she is out of desired rewards. One student is stealing from the treasure chest. Others are talking so much she begins to take away the tokens. A few other students always beg for tokens. A couple of her good students constantly ask to go to the treasure chest. She feels like she has created a monster system to bribe kids into acting how they are supposed to act in the first place.

Ms. Williams has indeed created a monster, and that is why *The Token Economy Playbook* has been written. Many well-intentioned teachers like Ms. Williams have tried to set up a token system and failed. The *Playbook* is written to minimize errors and increase the success ratio of a system designed to promote superior performance and personal growth.

CHAPTER 2

The Foundation

T oken economy systems are built on the foundation of sound behavior modification principles. From the works of such forefathers of the behavior modification approach such as Skinner, Homme, and Lindsley, certain principles have evolved that aid in accelerating learning and facilitating behavior change.

The major rules incorporating the basic principles of behavior modification include:

1. Keep the law of reinforcement firmly in mind throughout the day .
2. Reinforce a child when he exhibits desirable behavior, and ignore him when he exhibits undesirable behavior.
3. Use positive reinforcement rather than punishment.
4. Reinforce desirable behavior immediately.
5. When first modifying a behavior, apply a continuous schedule of reinforcement; later, after the behavior is acquired, gradually shift to an intermittent schedule.

6. Make high-probability activities contingent on the performance of low-probability activities.
7. Use the principle of pairing to expand your range of effective reinforcers.
8. Reward approximations toward the desired response.
9. When an action is desirable under specific circumstances, it should be reinforced only under those conditions.
10. If a behavior that has been reinforced to a high operant rate is no longer desirable, it can be extinguished by no longer reinforcing it.

1. Keep the law of reinforcement firmly in mind throughout the day.

Deibert[1] and Harmon (1970) provide a clear explanation of this basic law, or principle, of behavior:

> This basic law states that living organisms tend to repeat those behaviors that result in rewards (desirable outcomes) and tend to avoid those behaviors that fail to produce rewards. To state it another way, the "law of reinforcement" says: (1) Any behavior that is followed by a rewarding (desirable) outcome is likely to be repeated. The behavior is likely to *increase in frequency.* (2) Any behavior that is not followed by a reward will tend not to be repeated. The behavior is likely to *decrease in frequency. ...*
>
> To be consistent with the law of reinforcement we therefore have to assume that any behavior, which is repeated again and again, must be producing a reward (desired outcome). Otherwise, according to the law of reinforcement it will not occur. Only behaviors that produce rewards (desired outcomes) tend to be repeated. Therefore, if we observe a behavior occurring repeatedly, we have to assume that there is present in the situation some reward or desired outcome, which supports it. (p. 15)

---

1 Alvin N. Deibert and Alice L. Harmon, *New Tools for Changing Behavior,* pp. 15. Copyright © 1970 by Research Press.

According to the law of reinforcement, *behavior is learned as a result of environmental consequences.* Therefore, an effective way to change a person's behavior is to manipulate the environmental consequences, which immediately follow his actions.

2. *Reinforce a child when he exhibits desirable behavior, and ignore him when he exhibits undesirable behavior.*

This statement seems, at first glance, self-evident. You certainly would not intentionally encourage a child to perform an undesirable behavior by the use of positive reinforcement. (A reinforcer is an event that changes behavior. When a behavior is followed by a pleasurable event, the consequence is termed *positive reinforcement*). It is not likely you would want the rate of undesirable behavior to increase. However, the teacher without an adequate understanding of behavioral principles might unintentionally reinforce undesirable behavior. A common example is when a teacher argues with or pays attention to a child who exhibits undesirable behavior. The teacher, quite unaware of what is occurring, reinforces the child for displaying inappropriate actions since he manages to gain the teacher's attention.

What should a teacher do when a child exhibits an undesirable behavior such as playing with a toy during reading class? The immediate response might be to reprimand him. The teacher might consider this reprimand as punishment. Although it is aversive, the teacher is attending to the child, and the child may interpret the reprimand as positive reinforcement. Remember that the rule states "Reinforce a child when he exhibits desirable behavior, and ignore him when he exhibits undesirable behavior."

The natural question that follows is "What should I do?" The answer is to ignore him, and reward the child when he exhibits desirable behavior. To be even more effective, reinforce a behavior being exhibited that is incompatible with inappropriate behavior, while ignoring that inappropriate behavior. For example, a child who continuously gets out of his seat can be (1) reinforced for remaining in his seat; and (2) ignored when he gets out of his seat. The child simply cannot remain in his seat and out of his seat at the same time. We refer to this technique as the *double-barreled approach.*

However, there are occasions when the undesirable behavior may be potentially harmful to the child himself or to others and cannot simply be ignored. For instance, a child cannot be allowed to throw rocks at his classmates. In a case such as this one, it may be best to place the child in an isolated area for a short period of time. This technique, which can be used to handle potentially dangerous and persistent types of undesirable behavior, is discussed later along with other options.

3. *Use positive reinforcement rather than punishment.*

If a child is working to put a model ship together, he will work harder and put more effort into doing it correctly if he expects to receive a reward as a result. He will also take pride in his work. However, the child who builds a ship only because he knows he will be punished if he does not may do a poor job, will not enjoy the task, may attach negative connotations to ship-building, and will probably not like to build ships in the future. An analogy can be made from shipbuilding to learning academic and social behaviors. For example, a child might attach a negative connotation to doing arithmetic if he is punished nearly every time he does one or two problems incorrectly. Using the positive method is not only more efficient and productive in terms of the outcome, but is also more conducive to future activities along the same lines.

Punishment can be used to extinguish a response. However, punishment has been found in some cases to have undesirable side effects. If a child is punished, for instance, he may tend to avoid the punisher. Therefore, we strongly recommend the liberal use of positive reinforcement with little or no use of punishment.

4. *Reinforce desirable behavior immediately.*

Six-week reports, academic honors at the end of the semester, pins for citizenship, and promotions at the end of the year are often considered motivating devices for which children will strive every day of the school year. Is it reasonable to assume on the third day of school that a seven-year-old child will refrain from becoming angry at his peers who have been unkind to him so that nine months later he can get his name on a good citizenship roll? This example may be a slight exaggeration, but many parents, administrators, and sometimes even teachers expect a piece of paper received several months later (an extremely long period of time for a child) to be strong enough motivation to cause a child to exhibit desirable behaviors during those several preceding months. It is more probable that our angry little friend would avoid an argument if he knew that by *not* arguing, he would earn a cookie in half an hour. And would not the incentive to avoid arguing be even stronger if he knew he would get a token a minute or so later, that a token could be exchanged for a toy or something he really wanted?

Children need immediate feedback concerning their actions. Many times, when only a short time elapses before a child receives a reward, he may think he received the reward for one behavior, while in reality the teacher gave it to him for another. An example might be a teacher giving a reward to a child for completing his work several minutes after completion. Since the child was cleaning his desk during the few minutes immediately after he completed his work and before he received the reward, he perceived that he received the reward for cleaning his desk. As a result, the number of times the child cleaned his desk increased, while the teacher was actually interested in increasing the number of times the child finished his work. The child was confused, and the teacher lost faith in the system. This error could have been overcome by the teacher following the rule of reinforcing desirable behavior *immediately*. Intervening activities may confuse the child. While immediacy is not always feasible, adhere to it as closely as possible.

5. *When first modifying a behavior, apply a continuous schedule of reinforcement; later, after the behavior is acquired, gradually shift to an intermittent schedule.*

As the words imply, *continuous* refers to being reinforced every time, while *intermittent* refers to being reinforced every so often (not every time). In the beginning, to achieve "buy-in," it is best to reinforce immediately, every time, using a continuous schedule.

Information as to when continuous and intermittent schedules of reinforcement should be applied is presented on page 25. Reasons for shifting from a continuous to an intermittent schedule are also stated throughout the book.

6. *Make high-probability activities contingent on the performance of low-probability activities.*

A low-probability activity is one that a child generally would not want to do, while a high-probability activity is one that a child would like doing. The high-probability activity could never be considered a reward, whereas the low-probability activity would be the desired behavior the teacher wants the child to exhibit, but may be of low preference for the child. The major point here is that the reward, or high-probability activity, must be a strong enough motivator to get the child to exhibit the desired behavior. For example, a child is told he can play basketball for ten minutes *after* he completes ten arithmetic problems without an error. This principle is often referred to as the Premack principle. See Premack (1959; 1965) and Homme (1969) for more information on this very important and useful principle.

7. *Use the principle of pairing to expand your range of effective reinforcers.*

Some children will work long hours for rewards such as grades, stars, checkmarks, and tokens. However, in most cases, children desire these symbols or objects only after they have been associated with more basic or already learned reinforcers such as parent approval, privileges, candy, and toys. For example, a child who seems not to care what kind of grades he gets in school suddenly may become very concerned about his grades when told that he will receive five dollars for each *A* he earns. By pairing good grades with money, good grades became highly desirable to the child. This principle will be applied when discussing how to shift from a token system to a primarily social reinforcement system later in this book.

8. *Reward approximations toward the desired response.*

Generally, the appropriate response can be spotted and rewarded immediately, thus accelerating the rate of responses. There are cases, however, when a desired response is complex and involves several steps at once. A mistake at only one step may cause the end result to be incorrect. If a reward is provided at the completion of each individual step, the child will be better able to understand and perform the desired behavior required. It will also facilitate more efficient learning about the entire response. An example of this principle is the command for a young child to go outside. Involved in this process are at least five steps:

1. Going to the door;
2. Opening the door;
3. Stepping outside;
4. Closing the door;
5. Walking down the steps.

The child could be rewarded at each of these five steps.

In short, the principle involves rewarding small approximations toward the desired response, rather than withholding the reward until the child exhibits the complete response. This principle is sometimes referred to as *shaping*. It should be noted that individual variations of such characteristics as intelligence and age will determine the breakdown necessary for the performance of complex tasks. Further discussion of this important concept is included later.

9. *When an action is desirable under specific circumstances, it should be reinforced only under those conditions.*

Certain behaviors may be appropriate in one situation while not in others. This concept is often difficult for young children to grasp. An example of such a situation can be seen when a child goes to Grandmother's house. He gets reinforced for talking by Grandmother's approval behaviors, as well as by candy and cookies. However, when he attends church services, his talkativeness is considered undesirable behavior. When he begins to talk, he is not positively reinforced and may possibly even be punished. The child is, of course, in a quandary. In such a case, rule 9 should be followed—only reward the behavior in the specific situation in which it is desirable. After a few encounters with this type of reaction to his behavior, the child will begin to discriminate when talking is appropriate and when it is not.

Another, possibly even more efficient, means of handling such a case is to reinforce an opposing or competing response in the situation where the behavior is not appropriate. In church, if quiet behavior is reinforced, the talkative behavior will be reduced. The child cannot talk and remain quiet at the same time.

The next rule suggests what needs to be done when at one time the behavior is appropriate, yet at a later date the same behavior is inappropriate.

10. *If a behavior that has been reinforced to a high operant rate is no longer desirable, it can be extinguished by no longer reinforcing it.*

When a man drives a car with a stick shift, he is reinforced when he changes gears by the car moving along properly, taking him where he wants to go. However, when he trades his stick shift car in for an automatic car, he no longer needs to change gears the same way. It may even become undesirable behavior, since his transmission could be ruined. He will no longer be reinforced, the car will not move along properly, and may not take him where he wants to go. He stops trying to change gears—his "gear-shifting behavior" is extinguished.

A behavior that was reinforced was extinguished when reinforcement was not provided. In the classroom, a child who is beginning to learn numbers may be reinforced when expressing the concepts using his fingers. Later, however, as the child gains the ability to deal in abstractions, such use of the fingers might be considered undesirable. Reinforcement for using the fingers when counting can be withheld and finger counting will be extinguished.

Conclusion

Behavior modification principles have been applied throughout history. The precision with which an individual uses the principles should be critically considered. In other words, to modify behaviors in the most effective manner, the clue is precision. The principles discussed in this chapter are inherent throughout this book in explanations and suggestions.

The material presented in this chapter is not meant to be a comprehensive review of the principles of behavior modification, but an attempt has been made to give a brief introduction to some of the basic principles. An understanding of these principles is essential. In fact, the successful establishment of a token system demands understanding and skill in applying the general principles of behavior modification, as well as specific knowledge regarding token system implementation. *The primary purpose of this book is to provide specific knowledge about what is involved in the establishment of a token system; however, a prerequisite to successful application of applying the information presented is an adequate understanding of basic behavioral principles.*

CHAPTER 3

One on One

I t is best for the beginner to start using a token system with one student. It is simplistic, but it works to think of the token as praise; but the praise must be specific. Don't just say "Good job," or "Nice going"; say, "I like the way you are paying attention," or "You got them all correct." As you give specific verbal praise, you issue a token that can be exchanged for something the student wants, like a piece of candy, or an opportunity to lead the class out to recess, or a specific length of time to play a game.

Think of the token system as a means of communication—i.e., the student knows what he did to earn the token. The following are two real-life examples of using tokens with a single person.

CASE ONE: ALLEN

The dishwashing job was perfect for me. I was in charge of the kitchen: 30-foot by 30-foot cubicle. A row of three sinks lined the east wall; a state-of-the-art L-shaped stainless-steel Hobart dishwasher was installed next to the west wall. This dishwasher was an engineering marvel. Dirty dishes were loaded on a 3-foot by 3-foot square tray. The big stuff was sprayed off using a nozzle attached to a hose that hung from the ceiling. Once sprayed, the operator pulled up the left door, pushed the tray into the machine, then closed the door and pushed the "on" button. The machine did its magic. Once the machine cleaned and sanitized the dishes, the right door opened, and out came a piping hot tray. The dishes dried themselves.

I was fast as lightning. I kept up with every rush hour. I was so good I was promoted to the Fountain job my fourth week. At least, that's what I wanted to believe. The truth is the Fountain guy quit. I moved to Fountain, and a new dishwasher was hired. The Fountain was adjacent to the L-shaped stainless-steel Hobart dishwasher, but separated from it by the kitchen wall. During my high school years, after school, I had worked as a fountain jerk at the Sunflower Drug Store. Seen one fountain, you have seen them all. I already knew how to make shakes, sodas, and sundaes and draw soft drinks, so this position was a letdown: I was overqualified.

My success as a fountain jerk was short lived; by the end of the second week, I was moved to Garnish, like fruit basket turnover. I moved to Garnish, the dishwasher moved to Fountain, and they hired a new dishwasher. Ultimately, I moved from Garnish to Assembly, from Assembly to fry cook, from fry cook to grill man, from grill man to day manager, from day manager to night manager, and from night manager to the real manager, sometimes referred to as the head honcho—all in 9 months.

As the head honcho, one of my responsibilities was to hire and train the staff. I liked this assignment more than all of my duties. Not long afterward, I was approached by a placement counselor from the Division of Vocational Rehabilitation, with a request to hire clients who had spent their entire lives in an institution. It was during President Kennedy's administration, and he had launched a national initiative to hire the mentally retarded, now referred to as intellectually handicapped. I had no clue what I was getting into, but I agreed. Allen, the first Rehab client I hired, was 50 years old; he had never worked a day in his life and had an IQ of 52. I had no idea what a 52 IQ meant and didn't care. I wanted a dishwasher who would show up on time every day.

The first problem surfaced because Allen came to work on a bicycle and wouldn't leave it outside. He wanted to keep his eye on it. I was tolerant. I allowed him to chain his bicycle to my revered L-shaped stainless-steel Hobart dishwasher. I personally trained him how to run the Hobart. He could handle it except during a customer rush. When he got covered up, I'd run back to help him out. After a couple of months, he didn't need me.

I decided to hire another client from Rehab. His name was Kyle, in his 50s, and he wasn't as sharp as Allen. Now, two bicycles were chained to my Hobart. In the beginning, I assigned

Allen to teach Kyle. Later, when there was need, I moved Allen up to the Fountain, but this didn't work.

The problem wasn't with Allen; Allen was a good teacher. The problem was that Kyle just couldn't get it. He would forget to spray the dishes. He would forget to push the "on" button. As I worked with Kyle, I began to realize, the problem was: Kyle was retarded, very retarded. Allen and I both worked with Kyle, but he wasn't any better the third week than he was the first. As we began the fourth week, Allen came to me and suggested Kyle only spray everything, push the tray in the machine, and punch the "on" button. Allen would do everything else.

Allen may have had a 52 IQ but he was one smart cookie. By the second day, under Allen's tutorship, Kyle could spray, shove the tray into the machine, and push the "on" button, even during rushes. Without my saying anything, Allen had Kyle pulling the cleaned, sanitized dishes out of the machine. Next, he had Kyle sorting the china from the glass, and by the sixth week he had Kyle running the Hobart all by himself.

I moved Allen to Fountain and began using his training techniques. In the beginning, I only instructed him how to draw soft drinks. Once he had mastered drawing soft drinks, I taught him how to make shakes. After making that shake, I'd let him go into the kitchen and drink what was left in the bottom of the container. The second a person ordered a shake, Allen would make it Olympian fast so he could consume what was left. I added the techniques for sodas and sundaes one at a time. Before we all knew it, Allen was a certified, manager-approved fountain jerk.

Not leaving well enough alone, I hired a third client from Voc Rehab: Sam. Now, three bicycles were chained to the Hobart. Kyle trained Sam using Allen's training techniques, and within two weeks, Allen was training Kyle on the Fountain.

After Kyle mastered the fountain, I placed Allen at the Garnish table, but it was disastrous. Our routine was to place every sandwich on a bun. Garnish specifics written on the ticket were placed under the sandwich. The garnish person took the ticket, read the specifications and garnished accordingly. But Allen couldn't read, he couldn't even recognize letters. Garnish ingredients were identified on the ticket in letters: O for onion, P for pickle, T for tomato. Allen and I worked side by side, but he just couldn't get it. I called his counselor, and we sat down to discuss the situation. The counselor didn't know what to do. He told me I was the only employer who hadn't returned a client. In fact, I was the only employer who worked more than one client.

I decided to teach Allen letter identification using flash cards. I bought some three-inch-by-five-inch index cards at an office supply store. On each card, I'd put a letter in upper case on one side, and on the reverse side, I'd tape a picture of what the letter represented. During slow times, I'd sit down with Allen at the back table and drill him. He would get frustrated, fidgety, and anxious. Occasionally, he got mad—so upset he'd leave the table and go to the kitchen to sulk.

I needed something that would get him to focus, to try harder. I decided to use a shake as an incentive. After getting 10 cards correctly identified, I promised him a shake. I tried that token, but before he got the 10th card correct, he was in the kitchen sulking. The next session, before presenting a card, I made a chocolate shake, put a straw in it, and let him take a little sip every time he got a letter correct. I presented three cards. He took a sip of shake after every correct response. Then he reached over and pulled the stack of cards from me. He would take a card, name the letter represented, turn the card over to see if he was correct, and then sip the chocolate shake. When he misidentified an item, he would place the card to the side.

I sat there watching. Soon, he moved the shake right under his chin, put the straw in his mouth, and as he went through the cards, he took a sip when he got it right and moved the card to the side when he got it wrong without taking a sip. Right or wrong, the straw never left his lips. He did this for 15 minutes and never got mad or fidgety. We started to get busy, so we both had to go to work. He put the cards in his pocket and took them home with him.

The next day, I made a shake and we sat at the back table as before. This time, he went through the entire stack without making an error. He wasn't fast, sometimes he would look at a card for five, maybe ten seconds before he named the garnish, but he was always right, and he always sipped his reward.

Within a day or two, he could correctly identify each card as fast as I could. The card game transferred to the garnish table, except he was slow. He was always correct when garnishing each sandwich, but he was way too slow.

I remembered that after his shift, he would come to the register and buy five two-cent mints to take home. I liked those after-dinner mints myself and would consume one now and then on the job while no one was looking. I couldn't let him eat the mints at the garnish table, but I came up with the idea of placing a cup next to the table as a receptacle for pennies. When he garnished a sandwich correctly in a reasonable amount of time, I'd drop a penny in the cup and say "Allen, I like how fast you garnish."

I placed myself at the assembly position next to the garnish table. The assembly person's job was to take the garnished sandwiches, put them on a tray along with the specified drinks, and either shove the tray out the window for a carhop to deliver, or set it on the corner of the counter for a waitress to deliver. I wore a smock and filled one of the pockets with pennies. As I worked the assembly, I could easily supervise Allen. Every time he completed a sandwich in a reasonable amount of time, I'd drop a penny in the cup and say something like, "Allen, I like the way you garnish so fast." When things slowed down, Allen would empty the cup of pennies in his hand and buy some mints. Mints turned to candy bars, then bags of jelly beans, and ultimately to cigarettes. He would earn enough to buy anything he wanted. One time, he bought a cigar. He went outside around the corner of the building and lit up the stogie, much to the delight of the carhops.

Because of Allen, Kyle and Sam, I learned to master the techniques of breaking a task down into simple, easy-to-understand parts and ways to reinforce a completed task with shakes and pennies.

CASE TWO: MIKE

My greatest challenge was Mike. Mike was a tough kid, but I really grew to like him. He behaved himself in class, but we were told he was a terror in the community. A good employee, he liked his part-time job.

All of our students attended regular music class and gym. Mike didn't like music class. He behaved himself, but did not participate. Gym class was way on the other side of the school building, and we would have to drag him there. By the time we got him there and dressed out, the class was over. I talked with the gym teacher. He told me Mike would never participate like the other kids. The coach went on to say that Mike's older brother would never come to class. Even his dad had never come to gym class. The coach suggested it must be in the DNA.

The hallway from the special education classroom to the gym had six turns. So when the bell rang for gym, I positioned myself just around the first corner. All the other kids whizzed past me eventually; Mike rounded the corner. I jumped out at him, putting three tokens in his hand. I said, "It only took you four minutes to get here. Nice going."

I went back to my office, called the gym teacher, asked if Mike had arrived. Nope!

The next day, I waited around the first corner, and this time he came to the first corner in less than a minute. I jumped out, gave him three tokens, reached in my pocket for two more, and gave him a total of five. "Wow I didn't know you could move so fast," I told him. I went to my office, called the gym teacher. No Mike.

The next day. I positioned myself at the second corner. I don't know how fast he got to the first corner, but it took him five minutes to make it to the second. I held out three tokens in my right hand and took one of the tokens away and put it in my pocket. I gave him the two remaining tokens and said, "Five minutes, not bad, but disappointing." No Mike at gym.

The next day, at the second corner he beat all the other kids to that spot. He earned five tokens and a pat on the back. Still no Mike in gym.

Within a month, I had sucked him down into the locker room using token rewards, but I was exhausted. Now to get him to dress out. The school furnished socks and shorts, but no T-shirt. Since Mike always wore tennis shoes, it wasn't much of a trick for me to get him into the socks and shorts; the trick was the T-shirt. He didn't own a T-shirt, so we bought some and put them in the store. The T-shirts didn't sell very well, even when we dropped their price. Finally, we had a T-shirt giveaway for anyone who spent more than 25 tokens on a single day. Mike smoked, and cigarettes were 25 tokens each. It was like taking candy from a baby—he got his cigarette and a new T-shirt, and I got a chance to see him put it on.

Using tokens, I had been able to get him to the locker room and suited up just like the others, but I couldn't figure out how to get him to make it to class on his own without tokens. I gave up.

Not long after I gave up, Mike got in a fight as he was coming into school. He had been doing so well for so long. I was beyond disappointed—in fact, I was furious. He fought with a girl. Supposedly, she called him a name. Regardless of the reason, fighting was not permitted. Not surprised the principal called me to his office to get Mike. He explained his disappointment in front of Mike. He told me to handle it with Mike.

I grabbed Mike by the arm and escorted him to the track that circled the football field. I told him we were going to run laps until he dropped. (I don't know what made me do that.) Well, the two of us started running side by side. I continued to lash out at him verbally; I began to get tired. After the first lap, I ran a little slower than a trot. Next, I held to a fast walk, then a walk, then a stop. I dropped to my knees and rolled over to my side in a fetal position.

Mike never got more than five feet ahead of me. He stopped and looked back at me in my fetal position, and rushed to my side. He held my head in his hands and began to explain how sorry he was. Suddenly, he gently laid my head down and darted off. He ran and got the coach. With Mike on one side and the coach on the other, they took me back to my office. Mike even brought me a cup of water from the hall fountain.

That very day, I'm sitting in my office, somewhat embarrassed. The principal had said "The next time I tell you to take care of it, let the kid run, not you." He thought that was very funny.

My phone rings. It is Coach. He advised me to get down to the gym, Mike was suited up, participating. Down in the gym, there was Mike, leading the pack in calisthenics.

As the class left the gym floor to go to the locker room, I caught Mike and told him to come to my office after he dressed. Sheepishly, he entered my office and I motioned for him to follow me outside to the track. We walked the track to the far side and down the hill adjacent to the football field. Out of sight from the school, I sat down and then Mike sat down. I reached in my pocket, took out a cigar, clipped the end of it, licked the end, and lit up. Next, I pulled out a second cigar, clipped it, and gave it to Mike. Mike clumsily licked the end tip and put it in his mouth. I lit it for him. The two of us sat at the bottom of the hill and savored every puff. We never said a word. Finally, we discarded our cigar butts, and then he went to his part-time job in the community, and I returned to my office.

From that day on, Mike continued to suit up for gym and vigorously participated until the day he graduated. I learned that day, (and I'll never forget it), relationships are more powerful than tokens.

As a teacher fumbles through the process of using a token system, over time, the system becomes an automatic part of the teacher's repertoire. Eventually, the teacher knows when to use it and when to ease off. Along with praise and reprimand, a token system can be used for promoting superior performance and personal growth, but it is no substitute for trust and love.

CHAPTER 4

More than One

When using a token system, one on one, it is somewhat easy to tell if it works, when it works, and the degree to which it works. It is also relatively easy to modify or change behaviors immediately, on demand when deemed necessary. But when a token system is applied to more than one student or applied to one student in a group setting, things can go wrong in a hurry—even when the system is run by well-trained practitioners. Can it always be effective? Is it worth the effort and expense?

Soares (2011) set out to determine if, in fact, token economies, as reported in the literature, are effective. A meta-analysis was applied to 24 studies conducted in public schools. The results showed token economies did, in fact, increase academic readiness and decrease inappropriate behaviors.

A meta-analysis takes information from several studies and provides an opportunity to look at a big picture of results. It is an accepted method of summarizing the results of empirical studies within the behavioral, social, and health sciences (Kavale, 2001; Lipsey & Wilson, 2001). The design detects small or moderate relationships, obtains precise estimates of relationships, and finds patterns across studies (Gall, Gall, & Borg, 2006). Soares (2011) concluded that token economies positively affect behavior and academic readiness in both general and special education settings. Her findings are consistent with earlier studies (Klimas & McLaughlin, 2007; Salend, Tintle, & Balber, 1988; Sran & Borrero, 2010; Stevens, Sidener, Reeve, & Sidener, 2011; Truchlicka, McLaughlin, & Swain, 1998).

The duration of the studies ranged from four to 32 days. The majority of the studies worked with individuals or small groups from two to six students. Only two studies (Filcheck, McNeil, Greco, & Bernard, 2004; Salend & Lamb, 1986) worked with entire classrooms. Furthermore, there is no convincing evidence that children receiving token intervention in a self-contained classroom benefit more than those in a general education setting. This study suggests token economies are effective with all ages; however, the effectiveness is greater with older children.

What remains unanswered is whether token economies produce effects over long periods of time. Are the results long lasting, transferable, generalizable? Can token economies impact meaningful behaviors beyond basic academics and acting civil?

To address these concerns, *The Token Economy Playbook* lays out step-by-step procedures on how to implement a token economy in a classroom setting. It also reports a three-year study within an entire school (grades one to three) that morphed a typical token system into a currency-based system, where higher-level thinking and problem skills were introduced, and meaningful behaviors impacting personal growth were documented.

ANSWERS TO COMMONLY ASKED QUESTIONS AS INDICATED ON NUMEROUS OCCASIONS

1. *What, in general, is a token economy or system?*

A token economy in a classroom closely resembles the monetary reward system that operates in our free enterprise system. Students are rewarded (paid) for exhibiting behavior deemed appropriate by whoever is in authority. (The authority is the individual or group who regulates the reward and could be the teacher or even the entire class operating under democratic principles.) Just as in the adult world we receive money or other tangible rewards for doing what our supervisor or society expects of us, children can earn tokens for doing what the teacher or their peers expect of them. Just as money can be exchanged for goods, clothing, shelter, food, cars, and entertainment, tokens can be redeemed for items attractive to children.

2. What is the major difference between token and social reinforcement?

Under a token system, children who behave appropriately or achieve academically receive tokens, chips, checkmarks, etc., which are exchangeable (redeemable) for something tangible such as candy, toys, or pleasing activities. Social reinforcement, on the other hand, rewards children with attention, praise, kisses, and other displays of love and approval for exhibiting appropriate behavior.

Unfortunately, the dispensation of social reinforcers alone will not always produce change in children's behavior. If a child, because of a poor relationship with his teacher, does not care what the teacher says or does, attention and praise are not likely to be very effective in motivating the child to behave or achieve. Thus, it may be advisable in such cases to initiate a token system in the early stages of attempting to change a child's behavior. A child may be weaned from a token system to a social reinforcement system, if so desired, by combining social reinforcers with token reinforcers and very gradually employing more and more social reinforcers while supplying fewer tangible reinforcers.

3. What type of reinforcement schedule works best?

The terms *continuous* and *intermittent reinforcement* are common to the literature on behavior modification. However, information as to when these reinforcement schedules should be employed in a token economy is often hard to find.

A continuous schedule is in operation when a child is reinforced every time he exhibits the specified behavior. Although this schedule of reinforcement is applied frequently in laboratory experiments, from a practical standpoint, it is impossible to reinforce on a continuous schedule in the classroom. One teacher cannot observe and reinforce all the specified appropriate behaviors of all the children in a class unless only one or two children are enrolled. In the typical classroom, it is entirely likely that the specified behaviors could be exhibited and go unnoticed and thus lack reinforcement. Nevertheless, during the early weeks of a token program, the teacher should try to *adhere as closely as possible to a continuous schedule.*

The idea is to get the children succeeding. Later, the teacher will want to gradually shift to an intermittent schedule, in which reinforcement is not given after every response to maintain the behaviors acquired. There are two primary reasons for transferring to an intermittent schedule:

1. Behavior maintained by an intermittent schedule has a greater resistance to extinction.

2. An intermittent schedule is easier for the teacher to administer, since the teacher does not have to attempt to reinforce each child every time the appropriate behavior is exhibited.

4. *What is the reinforcer in a token economy?*

A reinforcer is the payoff that changes the child's behavior. In some instances, the tokens themselves will change children's behavior without being exchangeable for more pleasing items. Some children will work for gold stars, grades, or stamps. However, tokens usually become reinforcing only when they are paired and therefore associated with food, candy, toys, and other appealing items. When selecting items to serve as basic reinforcers, ascertain what is desirable and attractive. What appeals to one child may not appeal to another. If nothing is available that is attractive to the child, a token economy is not likely to change behavior.

One way of determining what a child likes is to ask. Another way is to record what each child buys with the tokens. The child buys most often what he likes best. A third way would be to construct a reinforcement menu and have the children select the items they would like to earn.

5. *What kinds of behavior should be of concern to the teacher?*

Most behavior modification programs have been concerned with disruptive behaviors. However, almost any type of behavior might be of concern. For example, reinforcing a student to say positive statements about himself might effect self-concept, while reinforcing conversations with others might improve interpersonal skills. In short, almost any behavior teachers and/or students consider appropriate can be fostered by a token economy.

Kuypers, Becker, and O'Leary (1968) wrote that one way to make a token system fail is to dispense tokens for meeting an absolute standard rather than for evolving improvement. Deibert and Harmon (1970)[1] state:

> Instead of expecting a child to perform a complex behavioral response on his first few attempts a *shaping* approach should be used. The task should be analyzed and an attempt made to determine the various steps or parts of which it consists. We then arrange these parts of the response in a series. We place them in a natural

---

1 Alvin N. Deibert and Alice L. Harmon, *New Tools for Changing Behavior,* pp. 34. Copyright © 1970 by Research Press.

order from the most basic or elementary part of the behavior proceeding through in step-wise fashion to the complete response. Each part requires a little more of the child than the one preceding. The child performs the first part of the response. After he is performing this part easily, we require the next step. Again, he is given time to learn this part of it well. Additional steps are required until he has been gradually shaped into performing the complex behavior or task. Of course, it is understood that each step or unit is followed by a reward. (p. 34)

6.   *What is the best way to observe behavior?*

In order to know if the frequency of a behavior has increased or decreased, you must know how often it has occurred in the past, as well as how often it is presently occurring. Behavior is primarily measured in terms of frequency of occurrence; that is, when a teacher evaluates a particular behavior, he counts the number of times the behavior appears. The counting usually takes place within a specified time interval.

To measure academic behaviors, formal and informal tests are often employed. For example, children are given an arithmetic test of ten problems to do in 20 minutes. The number of problems they get right or wrong is counted. Although social behavior is a little more difficult to observe, it can and must be done in order to know whether a particular behavior is decreasing or remaining stable.

To discourage a group of children from leaving their seats, the first step would be to count the exact number of times the children actually get out of their seats in a designated interval during any seatwork activity. It is advisable to count and record the number of out-of-seat behaviors two or three days before attempting to change the behavior. Hitting, shoving, pushing, speaking out of turn, sharpening pencils, crying, or almost any other observable behavior can be recorded in the same manner. The primary prerequisite for recording such behavior is that it be precisely defined in observable terms. Know exactly what you are counting. It may be advisable to count behaviors when children engage in the same type of activity each day. For example, they might display differing amounts of a specified behavior during reading than during physical education.

Remember to concentrate on only one or two behaviors at a time, unless you have a great deal of assistance and/or experience. The most unsavory types of actions can be dealt with first. Frequency should be measured before and after you attempt to change behavior; otherwise, you will have no way to determine whether the attempt was successful.

To illustrate what can be obtained by counting the behavior frequency during a specified time interval, take the case of Robert, a ten-year-old boy who continuously leaves his seat. In order to change this out-of-seat behavior, Robert's teacher decides to employ the token system—i.e., during a ten-minute interval, tokens are dispensed for *in-seat behavior*. On the first day, out-of-seat behavior is recorded without reinforcement to establish a baseline. Then, the teacher reinforces in-seat behavior while continuing to record the frequency of Robert's out-of-seat behavior each day during a ten-minute interval for the next four days.

He then constructs a graph (Figure 4.1 below) in order to have a clear picture of what changes in behavior were acquired. We see in Figure 4.1 that out-of-seat behavior for Robert occurred 20 times the first day without reinforcement, and then, five times the second day; five times the third; three times the fourth; and one time the fifth day with reinforcement. We can conclude that Robert's out-of-seat behavior decreased considerably during the five days under consideration.

In this illustration, we purposely decided that the teacher would observe for a ten-minute time period each day. But what if we had decided to have him observe various lengths of time each day? (A teacher might have various amounts of free time over a designated number of days.) It would then be useful to compute the rate at which the behavior occurs. The number of times a behavior occurs per minute can be easily ascertained by using the formula:

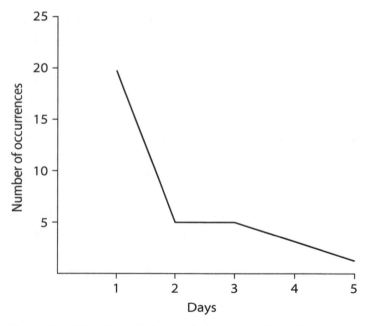

Figure 4–1. Out-of-seat behavior during a ten minute interval.

$$\text{rate per minute} = \frac{\text{number of occurrences}}{\text{number of minutes observed}}$$

If Susan is observed hitting Billy 30 times during a 15-minute time period, we could compute by this formula that she hits him two times per minute (2 = 30/15).

7. *When should tokens be dispensed?*

Tokens should be given immediately following the designated desired behavior. *A common mistake is to wait too long.*

When attempting to bring a child behaving inappropriately under control, it is sometimes very effective to reinforce someone near him who is behaving. This action lets him know in a subtle way he is missing tokens by continuing to act inappropriately. However, this practice requires extreme care. If the other children catch on, they might enter into an agreement whereby one child would consent to misbehave so that the children sitting around him will receive tokens. His fee/charge, of course, is a certain number of tokens from each child.

8. *What should be done about undesirable behavior?*

The two most common ways to handle undesirable behavior are to ignore it and punish it. When ignoring, do not argue or debate with the child; that is, pay no attention to him while he is exhibiting the undesirable behavior. Never, under any circumstances, give a token to a child who displays undesirable behavior. However, remember to reinforce *appropriate behaviors* immediately when again exhibited by the child in question.

An effective method of punishment employed to weaken undesirable behavior is the *time-out*. When a child acts inappropriately, he is told he will have to spend a certain amount of time, usually five or six minutes, in isolation. It is important to be specific: warn him that if he misbehaves during the isolation period, he will have to remain for extra time. The area designated as the time-out area should not be reinforcing and should be totally secluded. A completely bare room with only a light and a chair would serve best. Once you have put a child into the isolation area, be sure to continue to put him there every time he demonstrates the same behavior. **Consistency is essential**.

Another means of punishment is to take tokens away for misbehavior. We recommend this be done infrequently. It is much better to keep children working for positive reinforcement than to avoid a negative consequence.

Among the many possible inappropriate behaviors, two inevitably occur when a token economy is implemented. Sooner or later, a child will *ask for a token*. This behavior is inappropriate and should be treated as such. Another undesirable behavior occurs when a child tests the system by saying something like "I don't like those old tokens and I don't want any more." You should respond to these behaviors just as you would to any other undesirable or inappropriate behavior—by ignoring them completely. Remember, do not argue with, debate, or pay attention to the child exhibiting such behaviors.

9.   *Is there any particular way tokens should be dispensed?*

Certain procedures should be followed. Go to the child, and place the token in his hand or on his desk. Do not have the child come to you. At the beginning of each new activity, dispense a large number of tokens, and gradually decrease the number being given after the child is under control. Smile and have physical contact with the child: place your hand on his shoulder and smile. In the initial stages, say aloud the reasons for dispensing the tokens so that every child in the room will be fully aware of the reasons. Make your sentences clear, concise, and to the point: "I like the way you are sitting quietly." Do not use unnecessary verbiage such as "Here is a token because I like the way you are sitting quietly." Occasionally, socially reinforce a child without dispensing a token. These last three procedures will make it easier to shift to a social reinforcement system.

10.   *Should the children be allowed to play with the tokens they have earned?*

There is no real harm in allowing children to see and touch what they have earned during the first day or two of a token program. This activity seems to make the tokens more valuable to them. However, playing with their tokens beyond the initial stage can be a problem. They might tend to manipulate their tokens when they should be attending to a specific task. Rewarding those children who keep their tokens off the top of their desk and out of the way will normally stop this type of activity.

11.   *What should be used for tokens?*

Heavy or awkward objects should be avoided. While it makes little difference what is used for tokens, it is important they be attractive, lightweight, durable, easy to handle and dispense like poker chips or buttons. Because a large number of tokens may be dispensed to each child, ease of handling is especially important.

12. Will children steal tokens from each other?

Most children will not steal. If a child is suspected of stealing, tokens of a unique color can be awarded to him. When the children exchange their tokens for basic reinforcers, this child should turn in only tokens of the same color dispensed to him. His stealing will probably diminish when he finds there is nothing to be gained. One alternative to using different colored tokens would be to let the child steal. Other children will learn very quickly to make provisions to protect their own tokens.

13. Should tokens be dispensed on a group or individual basis?

When a group of children have the ability to perform equally well on a particular task, reinforcing them as a group would be appropriate. Children, however, often differ in their abilities, and the dispensation of tokens should be individualized, just as instruction should be. Regardless of the performing level of an individual child, he should be given a token when he makes improvement.

A note of caution should be added here. If you reinforce children on a group basis, it is essential to be absolutely sure that every child in the group has exhibited the behavior being reinforced. Since it is almost impossible to observe each child, we strongly recommend that in most cases, you refrain from dispensing tokens on a group basis.

14. What is the best way to keep an accurate account of the number of tokens given to each child?

Efficient record-keeping procedures can save time and trouble. There is probably no one best way to do this, but several methods appear to be fairly efficient. One is to have your aide (if you have one) count the number of tokens earned by each child at the end of each day, and enter the number on a recording sheet. No aide? You will have to take five or ten minutes at the

Name	Mon.	Tues.	Wed.	Thurs.	Fri.	Total
1.						
2.						
3.						
4.						
5.						
6.						
7.						
8.						
9.						
10.						
11.						
12.						
13.						
14.						
15.						
16.						
17.						
18.						

Figure 4–2. Recording sheet for number of tokens earned.

end of each day to perform this task yourself. Most students can be taught to perform this task. Counting and recording the number of tokens earned can be a practical learning experience. Figure 4.2 below illustrates how a recording sheet may be organized.

15. How many tokens are normally dispensed in a regular school day?

It is better to dispense too many tokens than too few, especially at first. Your objective is to encourage the students to behave and achieve as soon as possible. Most people, for some reason, tend to be stingy with the tokens—they hoard them. It is imperative to give out large numbers of tokens: 25 tokens for each child on the first day is not excessive. Search out appropriate behavior. Catch children being good, and reward them immediately. To ensure that you do not end up hoarding tokens, learn to forgive—and do not hold grudges. If a child displays undesirable behaviors at ten o'clock one morning, do not ignore him for the remainder of the day. He should be watched carefully and rewarded immediately when he exhibits appropriate behavior. In this way, he will begin to work for tokens rather than spend the entire day challenging the system by displaying undesirable behavior.

16. How can I dispense tokens and teach at the same time?

It would be foolish to pretend that dispensing tokens is not a difficult task. Nevertheless, it can be done successfully. The use of a timer can help make the job possible. Almost any easy-to-handle mechanical device that can be set to ring at random intervals (averaging five to seven minutes) can be used as a timer. When the timer rings, you can stop whatever you are doing and dispense tokens to those children who have exhibited appropriate behavior *during* the preceding time interval.

Another way—easier and more efficient—is to have your aide dispense the tokens. The aide should be specifically instructed when, and for what reason, to dispense tokens. Also, if you arrange your classroom so that you can see most of the children most of the time, your job will be much simpler.

If it is not feasible for you to dispense a minimum of 25 tokens per child per day, then do not attempt to establish such a system in your classroom.

An alternative to a token system could be a contingency contract system.

17. What is a token economy store, and with what should it be stocked?

A store is exactly what its name implies. It could resemble on a small scale any real store stocked with a wide variety of items: perfume, candy, lotions, jewelry, lipstick, combs, crayons, pencils, paper, magnets, and balls. Almost anything attractive to children might be included, which is the most important aspect to consider. Of course, safety, practicality, and price of the merchandise must also be taken into account.

It is best to stock the store with edible items in the initial stages. A small chocolate candy bar, for instance, can be consumed on the spot, quickly providing immediate reinforcement. As a result, the child learns rapidly that the basic reinforcers are worth achieving. A toy, which cannot be played with until after school, does not provide the immediate reinforcement that consumable items do.

18. What is all this going to cost in cold cash?

Surprisingly, the establishment of a token economy is not as expensive as most people might think. The actual expense will depend on the characteristics and backgrounds of the children being served—especially their ages and socioeconomic levels. We have found that in most cases, a store can be adequately stocked for 15 to 20 cents per child per week. For a group of 15 to 20 children, a classroom can operate a token economy for as little as a three-dollar initial store outlay, plus $2.25 per week operational cost. A teacher with good community relations can usually defray a large portion of the cost through actively seeking donations from various businesses, organizations, and clubs. Basically, the actual cost of a token system is directly related to the number of tokens charged per item, which is determined by the amount of money you have to spend.

19. How many tokens should be charged for various items?

The number of tokens charged for an item should be directly related to the cost of the item. Adequately stocked stores have a wide variety of merchandise that sell for a penny to a dollar or more. A quick and easy method to determine token cost per item is to add at least one zero to the actual cost of an item. Under this system, an item costing a penny would be worth ten tokens, and a five-cent item, 50 tokens. A 50-cent bottle of hand lotion would be worth 500 tokens. These prices are only examples. The number of tokens charged for each item should fit your own budget and situation. A precise method for determining token cost per item can be found by using this formula:

$$\frac{\text{Number of children in class} \times \text{Estimated tokens dispensed per child per day} \times \text{School days per week}}{\text{Amount of money the teacher has to spend per week (in cents)}} = \text{Number of tokens to charge per penny}$$

A teacher knows the number of children in his class, the estimated number of tokens to give out per child per day, the number of school days per week, and the amount of money available to spend per week. It is therefore a simple arithmetic calculation to figure the token cost per penny. For instance, let's say a teacher has 15 children and plans to dispense approximately 50 tokens per child per day, has a five-day school week, and has $2 to spend. The teacher can figure the token cost per penny in the following manner:

$$\frac{15 \times 50 \times 5}{200} = \text{no. of tokens to charge per penny}$$

$$\frac{3750}{200} = 18.75$$

In this example, the teacher would charge 19 or 20 tokens per penny; i.e., a penny piece of candy would cost 20 tokens, a five-cent candy bar would cost 100 tokens, and a 50-cent jack-ball set would cost 1000 tokens.

Regardless of the method used for figuring token cost per item, a record should be kept of what each child buys, in order to determine what is selling and what is not. In this way, you will not buy a lot of merchandise that does not appeal to children. However, no matter how careful you are, you will sooner or later buy some things the children do not want to purchase at the price you are charging. If it is apparent that an item is not selling well over a period of time, hold a sale where these particular items sell for two-thirds or one-half the tokens normally charged.

In addition to sold merchandise, there are many items that could be rented: CD players, tape recorders, radios, and various games. Johnny might be allowed to pay 30 tokens to rent the CD player for 15 minutes. Time to engage in a highly desired activity such as playing basketball outside for ten or 15 minutes can also be sold.

We would like to make it perfectly clear that it *is* possible to operate a token economy at almost no cost. Activities, items, and privileges can be used and rewarded at no cost to the teacher or school district. Free items and privileges that have been successfully used by teachers are extended recess, running and yelling, field trips, eating lunch in the classroom, tutoring younger children, and feeding the class pets. Many teachers implement token systems at no cost by using such rewards.

20. How often should redemption of tokens occur?

Redemption of tokens should probably take place once or twice each day during the first three or four days of a token economy. In this way, the children are made aware of the real value of tokens shortly after receiving them. However, a goal of opening the store once a week should be slowly established. The children can afford to redeem their tokens more frequently during the first week because a large number of tokens (as many as 25 to 75 per day) should be dispensed to each child during the earlier stages of a token economy. This number is gradually reduced until it stabilizes at approximately 15 to 30 tokens per child per day. (The numbers quoted are what we have found to be about average; the actual number will vary from one program to another and from one child to another.)

Two events happen frequently enough in relation to redemption of the tokens to warrant special attention. First, nearly every child will sooner or later ask to go to the store at an unscheduled time. If this is allowed, other children will be asking to go soon afterward. Remember that when you answer such a question in the affirmative, its frequency will tend to increase. If you do not want to reply to this question frequently, simply say no. Second, children will ask if they can save their tokens. This certainly does no harm, and may result in some interesting learning. In fact, we imagine that children can learn to "put something away for a rainy day" when becoming responsible for the tokens they spend and save.

21. *Why bother with the establishment of a token economy?*

When inappropriate behaviors have been reinforced over a long period of time, a concrete, clear, and precise system of communication is needed when attempting to make a radical change. In addition, when a student, for whatever reason, does not trust authority figures, he sometimes will tend not to hear what they say—even what is positive. Tokens are a highly visible means of communicating to the child that appropriate behaviors will be rewarded.

Some students exhibit what seems to be at first glance such a low frequency of appropriate behaviors that praise and attention can be hard. When employing a token economy, if you end the day with one child having only two or three tokens, you know to watch the child more closely the next day and catch him exhibiting appropriate behavior. If each child does not have the minimum of 25 tokens, you have done a poor job.

Finally, the implementation of a token economy helps train you, the teacher, in the precise use of behavior modification principles. You must focus attention on appropriate behaviors while ignoring undesirable behaviors.

22. *Should social reinforcers be used in conjunction with tokens?*

Yes, combine verbal praise and attention with tokens. After children learn appropriate behaviors via a token system, most teachers attempt to wean them away from tokens and toward social reinforcement. If praise, attention, and other displays of approval have been combined with the dispensation of tokens, the move from a token to a social reinforcement system will be easier.

CONCLUSION

The foregoing questions and answers are not meant to be comprehensive. However, they provide clues as to the practical issues involved in the successful implementation of a token system. Keep the following points in mind.

The establishment of a token economy is not a substitute for good teaching. Nor is it a panacea for all education problems. It is a tool that can help shape behavior. When employing a planned behavior modification approach, interesting, exciting, and meaningful lessons should be geared to the ability level of each child. If children are required to learn dull and meaningless lessons under a token system, this would misuse the system.

Token systems can be implemented for one child, a specific group of children, or an entire class. Of course, the larger the number of children involved, the more assistance is needed for dispensing tokens, evaluating behavior, and keeping records.

Although some consider the operation of a token economy impersonal and cold, the benefits gained can allow the teacher to be very warm and human. Disciplinary problems, which sometimes lead to strained relationships between teacher and student, are reduced.

Token reinforcement is a powerful tool; it can create as well as solve problems. Both you and the students must know exactly what behavior you are reinforcing.

The following incident occurred the first time one of the authors participated in a token system. After dispensing tokens for approximately 15 or 20 minutes, he noticed that nearly all of the children were raising their hands, getting out of their seats, and tiptoeing back and forth to the pencil sharpener. He had given a token to a child for raising his hand and asking to go to the pencil sharpener. After the child quietly went to the pencil sharpener and back to his seat, he was given another token. The other children caught on quickly. In a few minutes, to the teacher's surprise, he observed the entire class tiptoeing back and forth to the pencil sharpener. The successful establishment of a token economy calls for industry, patience, knowledge, and skill. Nevertheless, it has been our experience that when used with some degree of consistency, the results are most gratifying.

CHAPTER 5

Step-By-Step Procedure

Often, when a teacher is interested in implementing a token system, he must rely on haphazard guessing as to how to set up his program. He knows children must be reinforced, and reinforcement must be meaningful, but what he does first or second in developing the program is left to sheer intuition. Our objective in this chapter is to present a step-by-step analysis of how a token system can be implemented. This is only one method; as in most programs, there are several ways to proceed. However, this method has worked, effectively and efficiently.

This chapter is divided into two sections. Nine steps that should be taken before establishing a token economy are presented first. The second section consists of day-by-day procedures that can be followed when actually implementing a token economy.

Steps Before Implementation

1. *Become familiar with behavior modification generally and token systems specifically.*

Before an individual sets out to do any job, including implementing a token system, it is helpful to learn how it is done. The teacher can learn from experienced professionals. We assume you are reading this book to learn about a token system; remember to read its entirety before implementing such a program. In addition to this material, you should read about behavior modification programs others have established and understand the problems encountered. Abstracts and descriptions of articles and books containing such information are provided in Chapter 12. Reading Chapter 12 can aid you in choosing literature applicable to your particular situation. Read the original sources that interest you the most.

Another source of information might be classes in your school system or in surrounding cities and counties in which token programs have already been established. Talk to the teacher, watch the system in operation, and if the opportunity presents itself, get involved by such means as distributing tokens to experience the system firsthand. Remember, read and learn as much as possible before attempting to establish a program yourself.

2. *Arrange the setting for effective and efficient implementation.*

Arrange to provide a conducive atmosphere for the activity. The best way to determine the correct arrangement of your classroom is to consider what activity needs to be carried out. Set up the room accordingly. Since the teacher must be aware of each child's actions at every moment, position your desk so that you can see each child. Small meeting areas as for reading groups should be set up so that you can easily see the remaining children while conducting such meetings. This warning may seem a bit trite, but many teachers work in small groups with their backs to the remainder of the class to help eliminate distracting sounds or movements. If tokens are going to be dispensed for appropriate behavior, then the teacher must be able to observe as much behavior as possible.

The ability to see the children should also be considered when writing on the board. Try to put all needed information on the board before the school day begins. A computer hooked to an LCD that projects images on a screen is invaluable when implementing a token system; however, if such equipment is not available, a large mirror can be mounted high on the wall to help the teacher observe the class.

Another necessary aspect for the proper implementation of a token system is immediate reinforcement of appropriate behaviors. The aisles and desks should be arranged so that any point in the room is quickly and easily accessible. The student should not have to wait for reinforcement.

Take these considerations into account. As you read the principles and techniques presented throughout this book, other modifications of the classroom setting will become apparent.

3.   *Obtain appropriate tokens.*

Tokens are those objects used as immediate reinforcers for appropriate behavior exhibited. They usually have no intrinsic value; however, they take on value when exchanged for desirable objects—the same as money. The token is the form of currency employed in a token economy.

Like money, tokens should not be easy to duplicate. If they can be easily duplicated, forgeries will begin to appear in the classroom, and your system will break down. Children will no longer need to display the appropriate behaviors to acquire their currency.

The number of tokens needed will range anywhere from 1000 to 4000, depending on the size of the class. If you estimate 100 for each child, you can be reasonably assured you have an adequate number, assuming the children turn in their tokens at the end of each day, with credit being given for tokens earned.

Alternatives to using tokens is a card taped to each child's desk or the use of an individual notebook. On the card or notebook, you can make a tally mark each time the child displays an appropriate behavior, thus eliminating the need to carry a large number of tokens. This setup should have the same applicable characteristics of tokens. One advantage of tokens, though, is that the child has tangible, manipulatable objects to show for appropriate behaviors. For some children, this concreteness appears important. Remember, as the teacher, you are in the best position to make the decision as to the type of tokens to be used.

4.   *Establish your store.*

The store incorporates the process of token exchange. The teacher must consider what items will be available, the price of the items, store hours, placement, and bookkeeping procedures. The quality of the store will determine the strength of the system. The more desirable the store items, the harder the children will work to obtain them. Since the items supply the motivation for the children, their selection of these items is extremely important. What is highly reinforcing for one child may be of little value to another. Careful observation of each child's purchase should, therefore, guide the purchase of items.

Other considerations include the amount of money that can be invested and the availability of inexpensive items. We suggest that the teacher explore every possibility for obtaining free items and financial assistance. Also, renting items already available in your classroom can be substituted for merchandise such as coloring space, time to use an iPad or smartboard, or even personal computer time for short periods of time during the day. These rentals will expand the selection at no cost to the system. In the beginning, many inexpensive items should be available in the store so the children will not have to wait. After the children have begun to reap the benefits of the program, higher-priced items can be made available, and the children can begin to save their tokens to purchase these items.

The store can be presented in several ways. The teacher may conduct the store from his desk or from a table in another area of the room. A decorated box can be used as a distribution center, or items may simply be displayed on any flat surface. Children enjoy an attractive arrangement and colorful price list; however, any arrangement that is efficient and effective can be employed. Initially, the store should be open quite often, while in the latter stages, more time can elapse between openings. This scheduling aids the children to profit in the beginning.

Bookkeeping procedures, although they appear to be secondary, are important. After the first few days, children tend to start saving, and, in some cases, hoarding their tokens. Since the children cannot keep all the tokens they collect (say, over a week's time), a precise system of record keeping, similar to a banking system, must be set up to list the number of tokens received each day. If the students were allowed to keep all of the tokens, many would be lost, some possibly stolen, and the economy itself might collapse. After a short time, no tokens would be available for continued distribution. Haphazard accounting of these tokens is quickly recognized by children. Naturally, they would rebel, since they would not be receiving the due benefits of their efforts.

Along with the banking system, other recording procedures need to be devised. Information concerning items purchased, purchase price, and the purchaser should be systematically recorded. Such lists can identify what items are more desirable to an individual child, as well as which items are generally reinforcing for the class as a group. A list of items purchased and the prices of things bought can help estimate the amount of money and number of items needed for the store each week.

The store is an extremely important component of the entire token system. It is time consuming and can be tedious, but if conducted properly, its benefits will quickly become apparent.

5. *Collect other necessary materials.*

When implementing a token system, many teachers overlook the problem of making tokens easy for the children to handle. After a child receives four or more tokens, the problem arises of losing tokens, their tokens falling off the desk, or even being played with at inappropriate times. Although these problems pose no real threat to the system, they can become a distraction and annoy the children as well as the teacher. Prevention is simple. For example, provide each child with a box, small bag, or cup into which the tokens can be dropped at the time when received.

Yes, the children need containers for tokens, but you also need some carrying aid for the large number of tokens to be dispensed. In order to keep hands free for other necessary tasks, you could wear some type of container on or around your clothing: an apron with pockets, a money pouch, an old purse with a shoulder strap, or clothing with large pockets. Whatever is most comfortable and accessible should be used.

Devices such as these can be used to save time and energy. One caveat: be reasonably sure precision is enhanced.

6. *Develop a set of rules for your class.*

Rules have always been a classroom necessity, whether oral or written, vague and long-range or specific and short-range, and behaviorally oriented. This last type of rule should be used in the classroom. Rules should be clear and unambiguous, written so that the children can easily understand the behaviors deemed appropriate and specifically stated in measurable terms. An example of a poorly stated classroom rule is "Practice good citizenship in the classroom." A child may feel he is fulfilling his obligation if he salutes the flag in the morning, despite the fact that he kicks the child in front of him. Citizenship undefined is extremely abstract and very difficult to measure.

Another type of rule to avoid is "Don't kick your neighbor." Although this rule focuses on a particular action, is specific, and can be measured, it is expressed in the negative. Stating the rule in negative terms implies an expectation the child will display the inappropriate behavior—and children live up to expectations. A better phrasing would be "Keep your feet under your own desk when seated." This rule focuses on one particular action; it is specific, can be measured, and is framed in the positive. If the child's feet are anywhere but under his desk, he is breaking the rule. It is also unambiguous. It points to appropriate behavior, rather than what is the inappropriate behavior.

The rules provided should determine the behaviors to be reinforced. Only a few rules should be developed in the beginning; it is not feasible to change a large number of behaviors in the first few days, unless you have lots of assistance or expertise in applying behavioral principles. Focus on a small number of behaviors that can be easily handled. When these have been adequately modified, move on to a few others. When including additional rules, remember to follow the criteria in stating them: make them clear, unambiguous, measurable, and positive.

7. *Determine the specific behaviors of individuals that require modification.*

The rules have been set. You are nearly ready to begin. But are you? Working in the field of education, you are frequently reminded of the individual differences among human beings. In the classroom, these differences may very well span the physical, social, emotional, and intellectual. As a result, rules for the whole class may not meet the needs of individuals within the group. To meet the needs of each child adequately, take into account their individual characteristics. Rules must be adjusted for specific individuals in order to enhance their growth and to promote a conducive classroom atmosphere. For example, one child may beat his head on his desk when he is upset. It would not be plausible to develop a rule to modify this inappropriate behavior for the entire class, but such a detrimental behavior should not be ignored. Consequently, a rule should be formulated whereby this particular child can be reinforced when he keeps his head away from his desk, although it is not necessary to reinforce others for the same reason.

Initially, you should not attempt to modify every behavioral problem of every child in your classroom. Begin with a number that can be easily handled. Change the most severe first and gradually address others.

8. *Collect information concerning behaviors exhibited related to the rules formulated.*

Before an objective judgment of behavioral change can be made, we must know what the behavior was like before modification was introduced (the baseline). After the rules are made that specify the appropriate behaviors desired, make a list of them. Whenever the opportunity arises, tally how many times you see the appropriate behavior being exhibited during a designated interval. This tally will provide a comparative base for later observations after the modification attempts have been incorporated. There will be no need to tell people about the change in your students; you can show them.

9. *Secure help.*

By now, it has become quite apparent that a token system program is time consuming and requires a concentrated effort, especially in the initial stages. Because of the amount of time required, we believe that outside help should be secured if a teacher's aide is not available. The program can be carried out alone, but unless you are very familiar with behavioral principles, help is essential.

You may be able to find a volunteer who can be available during the initial stages of the program (approximately ten days). If, for some reason, the volunteer is not available for training as well as during support time, another volunteer must be secured and trained, thus creating more work for you.

If at all possible, the volunteer should not be a class member's parent or anyone otherwise involved with the students, since objectivity is a major prerequisite. Any emotional or social involvement with certain members of the class may result in partiality and contribute to the breakdown of the system. All children must have an equal chance to earn tokens based on the overt behaviors they exhibit. Three possible sources of such impartial volunteers might be civic organizations, college students, or community action groups.

The aide or volunteer must be trained in behavioral principles, the goals to be achieved, appropriate ways of reacting to different situations, and methods for dispensing tokens. The volunteer's main jobs will consist of helping in the dispensation of tokens, operating the store while you work with the class, and being available to help individual children with problems like counting tokens until the children become adept within the system. The most difficult task to learn, which must be stressed in the training process, is to become objective with the program.

When the initial hurdle has been achieved—hooking the children onto the system—less help will be required, and the volunteer can gradually be phased out of the classroom.

Day-by-Day Procedures

1. *The first day.*

The first day you introduce the program into the classroom will be a rewarding venture for you, as well as for the children. Even before the verbal explanation, excitement will be high on the part of the children as soon as the store items are seen.

At the beginning of the day, set aside time for explaining the entire program. Show the tokens to the children, and describe how they are to be handled at their seats. Display the items for which the tokens can be exchanged. Also include a discussion about the cost of the items, and how the exchanges will take place. Above all, discuss the rules and expectations in relation to the rules. If a new adult (aide or volunteer) comes into the classroom at this time, he should be introduced and his presence explained. Children cannot be expected to become adequate participants in a game unless they know the rules and how to play that game.

To each child, give a cup, a rubber band, or any container that will be used to store the tokens earned. Academic activities should be conducted in the standard manner. The only major change from the regular classroom procedure should be the dispensing of tokens for appropriate behavior exhibited.

A schedule of continuous reinforcement should be applied; the children should receive a token for every designated appropriate behavior they exhibit. (Although it might be literally impossible to reinforce each child on a continuous schedule, you should come as close as possible.) You and your aide may have to surprise the problem child in the act of exhibiting appropriate behavior. Remember, try to give every child as many tokens as possible so they can become winners at the game and thus motivated to win more tokens—get them hooked.

In the middle of the day, the children should be given the opportunity to go to the store. Allow only one or two children in the store at one time. This takes more time, but eliminates headaches. Forms should be available at the store regarding items bought, costs, and purchaser. Let the children fill in the specified information; if necessary, you or the aide can help. Toward the end of the day, the store can be opened again. Set aside a few minutes during the first day to record the behaviors to be changed. These records can be compared to those taken during the baseline, as well as to records taken later on. In addition to recording behavior, take time before the end of the day to collect and record any tokens that the children want to save.

After school, discuss with the aide/volunteer the events of the day. Talk about more effective ways of conducting various activities. Review the rules for appropriateness, and then relax. Your most hectic session will be over.

2. *The second day.*

The children are already familiar with the system. If they won on the first day, they will be ready to start earning more tokens. Reinforce them for appropriate behavior from the time they enter the room, even before the formal school day begins.

Proceed in the same manner as the first day: follow your regular schedule, open the store, record behavior, and carry out banking procedures before dismissal. The only major change is one that deals with the store schedule. On day two, hold the store only once, and schedule it toward the end of the day. In this way, the children will begin to adjust to waiting a longer period of time before basic reinforcers are available.

3.   *The third day.*

Now that things have been going smoothly for two days, you may tend to relax. Don't. It is at this time that some children will begin testing the system. The children know by now that they will be automatically reinforced when they exhibit certain appropriate behaviors, but they will begin wondering if they can fool you into awarding tokens without displaying the necessary behaviors. They may even say, "You missed me, can I have my token?" This type of behavior is inappropriate and should be ignored. Never give a token to a child who asks for one. Be very careful what you reward. *At this point, precision is imperative.* The students may continue testing the system for a week or more, but if consistency is upheld, the problem will gradually disappear.

Continue with your schedule; however, delay the time the children can go to the store until the morning of the fourth day to help children delay gratification for a longer period of time.

4.   *The fourth day.*

The store should be held in the morning as a carryover from day three. Procedures should be implemented as usual. Also, as in day three, you should be especially watchful of children going through the testing stage.

5.   *The fifth day.*

The end of the first week is near—a major milestone. On this day, conduct the program as you did during the preceding four days. The store should be opened near the close of the day.

Evaluate the week's procedures. From observations and data obtained, behaviors that have been increased can be noted. Appropriate behaviors that have radically increased can be reinforced less often. Behaviors you wish to modify can be considered the next week. Modifications of these newly considered behaviors should not, however, be started until at least the second day of the second week, since you will need time to collect some baseline data.

From the information gathered concerning the store, you can determine which items appear to be most reinforcing. Base your selections for the following week accordingly.

6. *The second week.*

Introduce the use of the timer. Remember to explain the procedure to the children. A simple explanation might be "The timer will be used to help me remember to hand out tokens. Sometimes I get busy and forget to give them out."

Refine your techniques; if something doesn't appear to be running smoothly, seek a more efficient means of conducting that portion of the program. The store should only be held on Wednesday and Friday of the second week.

By now, the program should be showing signs of becoming an integral part of your class-room environment. The children—the most important component of that environment—can begin to have a more influential voice in what takes place. They can begin to be consulted concerning certain aspects of the program: for instance, input on stocking the items available in the store and suggestions concerning procedures and rules.

At the end of week two, evaluate the program. Include all recorded information, your subjective evaluation, objective observation data, observations of the volunteer, and the students' input. Consider these evaluations in planning the strategy for the following week.

7. *The third week.*

The program should be conducted as it was during the second week with two exceptions: (1) The store should be opened only once (on the last day of the week), which should become standard procedure for the remainder of the year. (2) A more complete transition from continuous to intermittent reinforcement should occur. The previously mentioned timer can be set to ring at periods of varying lengths. The range of time is usually from two to 12 minutes, averaging about six minutes. Children who exhibit the specified appropriate behaviors *during* any one interval can be reinforced at the end of that interval.

8. *The remainder of the year.*

By now, the program has become an integral part of your classroom environment. However, you should not relax. Continued evaluation and refinement must occur if the program is to remain in operation. Just as the wheels of a machine must be oiled and checked to keep it running at optimal level, so must the components of a token system. Allowed to become stagnant, they will disintegrate. Consistency, objectivity, and precision are as important after incorporation as during the initial stages.

Later on in the program, your workload can be somewhat lightened. Certain responsible children may be able to run the store or carry out the banking procedures. This should not, though, occur too quickly. The choice of students should be as objective as possible. If you continue to read the literature on token systems and are consistent in your evaluations, more ideas and innovations will occur to you, and a very productive year can result.

CHAPTER 6

The Currency-Based System

B y morphing the traditional token economy into a currency-based system, a quantum leap is taken into higher learning, problem solving, and more complex thinking. A currency-based system resembles a three-dimensional Monopoly game, where the school building becomes the game board and the play money is exchanged for actual goods and services rather than fictitious property and tiny wooden or plastic houses and hotels. The traditional token system is a method of teaching using behavior modification techniques to motivate academic performance and help with classroom management. While the currency-based system retains these pedagogical elements, the system itself becomes the curriculum.

The curriculum is a microcosm of real life: teaching empathy, buying gifts and privileges for others, delaying gratification, setting up layaway programs, establishing a safe deposit system in the school bank, and even character development when the emphasis is on honesty and fairness. As the currency-based system takes footing, the concepts of taxation and civic responsibility can be introduced, a strategy that increases the complexity of learning even more. Within a short period of time, the students can begin to run the system while the teacher monitors, advises, and counsels. The teacher takes on a role similar to governor or mayor.

Frankly, the interest in, and ultimately the establishment of, a currency-based system was stimulated by an anonymous reviewer's comment related to the book, *Establishing a Token Economy in the Classroom*:

> I find some difficulty in making an objective evaluation of this manuscript due to my bias about token economies in classrooms. I consider them to be a bad marriage between the process of taking candy from babies and outright bribery. I think they have about as much educational relevance as Dick and Jane. (Payne, Polloway, Kauffman, & Scranton, 1975)[1]

As indicated before, we believe a well-run currency-based token system provides an element of relevance to the classroom. Earned tokens are not bribery. Response cost, the technical term used for taking away tokens as a negative reinforcement technique, is not encouraged and only recommended for rare specific cases when administered by well-trained professional practitioners. The currency-based system is an attempt to deliver both teachers and students from "Dick and Jane" and the saber-toothed curriculum (Peddiwell, 1939) to an era of enlightened, real-life relevance.

How does the currency-based token economy differ from a regular token economy? Very simply, the currency is more realistic. Not only is it more relevant to the "now" of our society, but more importantly, it is realistic in terms of potential change. A currency-based token economy is real. Although a poker chip token economy can do many things, it adds an unnecessary air of artificiality to life in the classroom. For example, it is more realistic to charge $10 an hour for renting a basketball than it is to charge three blue chips, one red chip, and one white chip.

Poker chips or other artificial tokens are more than adequate for managing and motivating students. However, its realism makes the currency-based economy far more flexible in terms of achievement.

---

1   James S. Payne, James M. Kauffman, Edward A. Polloway, and T. R. Scranton, *Living in the Classroom: The Currency-Based Token Economy*, pp. x. Copyright © 1975 by Springer Science+Business Media.

Teachers need not feel that all the following suggestions are necessary to have a successful currency system. These suggestions point to what has been and can be done in extending the scope of the economy.

By employing a currency-based token economy, you can teach the traditional curriculum without being bound to traditional materials and textbooks. More importantly, this type of token economy creates *real* problem-solving situations in which children can test their perceptions, experiment with alternatives, and find new relationships and ways of being, becoming, and learning.

Addition, subtraction, multiplication, and division are taught both incidentally and directly. If a field trip costs $100 and John has only $72, he will quickly learn how much more money he needs to go on the field trip. If an item costs $8 and Jason gives the storekeeper $10, he will learn to expect change and to demand it if he doesn't receive it. And if an item costs $5 and Julie wants to buy three of these items, she will learn about multiplication. If three pieces of candy cost $9 and Debbie only wants one piece, the concept of division is inescapable. Teachers can expect the economy to become as sophisticated as your students' ability will allow.

An integral part of any token economy is the classroom store. The store may be as simple or elaborate as you and your students wish. Under the section "Answers to Commonly Asked Questions" in Chapter 4, question 17 on page 33 describes the basic store.

Elaborate stores, which may be operated or owned by students, may include management and pose problems such as the following:

wholesaling
warranties
complaints department
overhead
supply and demand
specials and sales
accidental spoilage and loss
shoplifting and theft
budgeting
employee-employer relations
advertising and display
returns.

As the currency-based economy grows, a classroom bank will be extremely desirable. Establishing a bank exposes students to savings accounts, checking accounts, large- and small-scale personal loans, small-business loans, and large corporate loans. Sophisticated banks will require a president and perhaps a clerk, whose salaries would be paid from the interest the bank receives. At this point, some students may observe a social and financial hierarchy developing: it is inconceivable to have a poor banker or a clerk who makes as much money as the president. Imagine the amount of math, reading, and writing—not to mention management skills—that are necessary to a bank operation.

Personal money management skills can be taught in conjunction with establishing the bank. For example, if John borrows $20 from the bank for one week at 50 percent interest, he will be confronted with the unpleasantries of usury. If he borrows $100 from the bank for ten weeks at 15 percent interest to buy luxury items and must repay that loan in weekly installments, he will learn the hard realities of installment credit, along with the benefits of "enjoy now, pay later." As the system becomes more complicated, John will obviously have to devise a budget to manage his money affairs.

Advanced classes may also organize a government to administer the classroom and elect a president, senate, congress, and department of justice. Officials can be appointed and elected, which will involve campaigns and advertising.

In a practical sense, the teacher may be establishing a limited democracy. Of course, the teacher is ultimately responsible for the class. Consequently, many final decisions remain the province of the teacher. It has been our experience that the teacher can usually manage the classroom without invoking martial law.

At this point, it should be obvious that a currency-based token economy is *real life*. Furthermore, it can be adapted to teach simple arithmetical operations as well as complex socioeconomic strategies.

One problem likely to occur in more developed economies is inflation. Classroom governments may need to impose wage and price controls. However, careful observation of supply and demand will often minimize this problem. Allowing inflation to pinch the children's budgets exposes them to the real problems faced in society today.

At some point, the opportunity to expand the currency-based token economy and the micro society to another classroom may occur. When this opportunity does arise, cooperation and joint planning are paramount. If two classrooms cooperate in a venture of this kind, the teachers'opportunities to teach will increase. In addition, mutual communication and regulation will be necessary, so classroom governments will need to address the problems of foreign diplomacy.

In teaching students about the problems of governments, the teacher may want to let them choose the type of government they wish to operate. Or the teacher may want to expose students to what it is like to live under a dictatorial governmental structure for a trial period. As you can see, this experiment could improve social and political institutions.

But what of the basic core curriculum of reading, writing, arithmetic, and spelling? How will you find time to cover the basics? Time is a precious commodity. The teacher can use time effectively in either an open or a more structured classroom approach. Learning basic skills is usually accomplished most efficiently in small-group or one-to-one teaching situations, challenging directive teachers to manage the rest of the class.

Thus, the major question is: "What do I do with those children I am not teaching directly?" This predicament is best resolved by using the open classroom design within the context of a currency-based token economy. Motivation for the acquisition of basic skills is accelerated by allowing children to earn money within specific learning activities. Students not involved in direct instruction may be engaged in activity centers, which can be student operated to a large degree. In actuality, then, the students control themselves, which gives the teacher time to teach. Many activity centers are designed and programmed to facilitate learning in the absence of a teacher. Although our purpose here is not to force a particular model of instruction on the teacher, we will offer suggestions from time to time on how to adapt the currency-based token economy to the open classroom concept in a way that will allow the directive teacher to "do her thing" if she so desires.

An open classroom offers many learning centers. The teacher guides student efforts in areas of interest. Learning centers can be expounded in terms of quantity and quality. A student can be *paid* to engage in learning centers that facilitate his development, or the child may decide to *purchase* entry into a center he chooses himself. In this situation, the child has decisions to make; at the same time, the teacher has a reasonable amount of influence over the situation. For example, if Fred, a kindergarten student, has mastered his color concepts and his numerical concepts to 2 and wants to play Candyland (a game that involves two to four players who know their colors and numerical concepts to 2), he may decide to pay $10 to enter the Candyland activity center. If Fred has poor eye-hand coordination, the teacher may offer him $10 to enter the paper-cutting activity center. Steven, on the other hand, needs to review his colors, but has good eye-hand coordination; he may have to pay to enter the paper-cutting center, but be *paid* to play Candyland. Under these conditions, the currency-based classroom involves existential choices on the children's part.

We believe, with Dewey (1938), that children learn by doing, and that time spent on making school life real is not lost. When students feel the need to learn and can see the logic behind education, the teacher needs less time to teach facts. We maintain that a currency-based token economy and a micro society are well suited to both the structured classroom and the open classroom. The money and the micro society blend into a workable alternative. A tremendous amount of activity goes on in the classroom because students are eager to acquire and apply the skills necessary for survival and change in today's world.

In the process, students may unfortunately pick up a skill that most of society would frown on: for instance, a black market may creep into a classroom. If you happen to sell candy in your store, you may find that at least one industrious, affluent student will begin bringing candy from home to sell to his classmates. If you allow this behavior to continue, you will not only bankrupt the store, but also teach your students indirectly that a black market is acceptable. If you legislate against the student's bringing candy from home, on the other hand, you may be punishing him for his creativity and initiative. One possible solution is to reward his creativity by guiding him into a more legitimate enterprise: allow him to set up his own store, but charge him rent for the space used and tax him for the goods sold.

Another problem that may arise is "sharking." If, for example, a student forgets to bring his pencil to school and consequently must borrow one from another student, he probably should pay the student a reasonable rent. There are times, however, when pencils are at a premium. Students wise enough to own several pencils can charge an exorbitant rental. A small amount of sharking is advantageous because it usually produces favorable results. But sharking can easily get out of hand, so be sure to guard against it.

 Loan sharking can also be a problem. A student may wish to buy something, yet have no money to do so, and his credit rating at the bank may be such that he can't get another loan until he pays a portion of his previous debt. In this situation, another student may lend the unfortunate soul a few dollars and charge him 100 or 200 percent interest. A good learning situation, but it is the teacher's responsibility to make certain it does not harm or traumatize the students. Use the situation to teach them a better way because these kinds of problems are realistic—indeed, many adults face them every day.

Two additional negative activities are goldbricking and featherbedding. It is easy—as well as appropriate—to set up time cards and pay the students an hourly wage for their work. The problem with this arrangement, however, is that a few students may become nonproductive when their pay is not contingent upon output. You may then find your classroom is becoming a welfare state. It is also possible that an older student will try to unionize his fellow students by bargaining for higher pay or an increase in staff but increase in production. Although this is realistic and reasonable, it can get out of hand. For instance, how would you deal with a strike? You might have to ask the classroom government to pass effective legislation. But remember, you are in charge. You have final responsibility. You control the purse strings.

These situations will not occur in the majority of classrooms because most students are not sophisticated enough to conceive of these ideas or follow them through. In a few classrooms, these problems do exist. Students functioning at higher levels need freedom to use their imaginations and apply the academic skills they have acquired. Your job is to allow them as much freedom as possible, encourage their ingenuity, and teach in an organized way so that the educational objectives of present and future life adjustments will be enhanced.

One advantage of the currency-based token economy is that parents can use it. As we indicated earlier, most parents will applaud and support its use. For example, one of our students had a severe case of strep throat that kept him home. He insisted his mother pick up some work for him and determine the rate of pay per unit of work. When the student returned to school, his mother expressed her amazement at how hard her son had worked at home and asked if she could use the currency system to pay him for making his bed and cleaning his room. After using the money system at home, she was delighted with the results and subsequently devised a token system that resembled a contingency allowance.

Principals have also used money successfully. One student was constantly running in the hallways. The principal tried various counseling and punitive approaches, with little success. He began using currency to reward the boy for walking, not running, and the boy's running was soon brought under control and remained so throughout the school year. As you can see, the successful use of money is not restricted to the classroom or to the teacher.

But we have learned from experience that it is generally unwise to have substitute teachers use the money in your absence. They have been known to give money non-contingently, arbitrarily refuse to give money, issue more or less money than is reasonable, and charge unreasonable prices for goods and services.

Some teachers have returned from extended leave, only to find the economy in a state of ruin. When one of the authors was ill and needed a substitute, he left detailed lesson plans for the substitute teacher so that there was absolutely no confusion about how the economy should be handled. When he returned, he found a pleasant note from the substitute, indicating that everything had gone well and she had thoroughly enjoyed herself. But later in the year, the same author again needed a substitute teacher, but unfortunately was unable to leave detailed lesson plans. When he returned, he found the store depleted of goods and the room in shambles. The substitute had issued $100 bills for $10 bills and had fined one student $1,000 for a $12 violation of the rules. In short, in one day, she had destroyed the entire system. It took more than a week to put it back together.

The currency-based token economy can be the key that opens the door to life in the classroom. Although there are many pitfalls in the implementation of a currency-based token economy, we believe the possibilities for excitement and the obvious relevance far outweigh the disadvantages. Classes should be alive, vivacious, relevant, real, dynamic, stimulating. At the same time, not all learning can be fun. Encountering new life situations always involves trial and error, vacillation, conflict, and anxiety.

CHAPTER 7

Goods and Services

A s previously indicated, when a teacher decides to use a token economy of any kind, she must have something to back up the tokens: in other words, the tokens must have purchasing power, or they will not work. To make the tokens valuable, the teacher must pair them with something that *students*—not the teacher—regard as reinforcing. How will the teacher recognize and secure appropriate reinforcers in advance? The students will often tell the teacher when asked, but the teacher can also find out simply by observing students' behaviors. If a student shows an interest in something without being forced, one can assume it can be used as a reinforcer.

In addition to asking students what they like and watching them to see what they do when given a free choice, a teacher can draw on her previous experiences. Actually, a game of probabilities is played when trying to predict what can be used as a reinforcer. The teacher can predict that certain activities, objects, and events will act as reinforcer, but it is the student who ultimately identifies the reinforcer by his behavior; the teacher can only make an educated guess. Most of the time, your educated guess will be correct; but if not, keep in mind that it is the *guess* that was wrong, *not the student*.

After spending some time watching students and identifying preferred reinforcers, the teacher will begin to recognize that students like some strange things. What most adults would regard as worthless may work for rewards. For example, children seem to love gadgets, whether they work or not. We have successfully sold watch parts. One item students always value is something they can take apart and look inside of, like an old watch or an old generator from a junked car.

Relics of your youth are an extremely valuable resource. Old balls, hats, bottles of perfume, and dolls can be put to better use in the store than in your closet. The resourceful teacher even asks other teachers and aides whether they would like their old treasures recycled.

Neighbors or acquaintances will often donate gentley used items:

Old neckties	Empty gift boxes
Old jewelry	Old giftwrapping
Old perfume	Old magazines
Old after-shave lotion	Old scarves
Empty tin cans	Empty Band-Aid boxes or other interesting containers
Old purses	Empty wine bottles for candles

A teacher can take advantage of free material available from companies as well as from government agencies. These free materials are given just for the asking; many have instructional value as well as reinforcing potential. Small businesses in the local community often dispose of items once they are no longer of value, things that children would love to get their hands on.

The following list of small businesses, along with some of their products or materials, will provide the class with many potential reinforcers. As you review the list, keep in mind to combine a childlike imagination with your adult ingenuity to visualize how some items might be used as reinforcers:

Advertising agencies. Art workups for ads are potential reinforcers. Many students are especially eager to buy original sketches or photos.

Air freight companies. Many boys are interested in pictures of cargo planes.

Aircraft dealers. Advertising pictures of small private aircraft are extremely interesting to children.

Airlines. Many major airlines have travel slogans and advertising material that children seem to enjoy. Brochures describing the kinds of planes the airlines use are also of interest.

Ambulance services. Stickers with the name and telephone number of the ambulance service sell well in the classroom store.

Architects. Old floor plans are big sellers among older children.

Art schools. Art students often have paintings that from an aesthetic point of view are worthless. Students seem to love them. An old painting, even if it is of poor quality, is a big seller.

Attorneys. Law books are frequently revised, and some attorneys are willing to donate their old editions. These books sell quickly in the school store.

Auto bearings. Worn-out bearings make wonderful "steely" marbles.

Automatic transmission repair shops. Old gears and transmission parts have a definite appeal for some students.

Automobile dealers. Many of the large advertising pictures are popular.

Bakeries. Bakers' hats and flour sacks are potential reinforcers.

Beautician suppliers. Free samples of hair spray, cream rinses, and shampoo are often available.

Bicycle dealers. Advertising pictures of many different types of bikes, and especially accessories, are good items.

Blueprints. Old blueprints seem to appeal to many children.

Boat dealers. Many times, boat dealers have large advertising displays and pictures, which they will donate.

Boot makers or cobblers. Pieces of scrap leather are always highly prized by students.

Bowling alleys. Often, bowling pins become chipped or dead and are thrown away. The pins can be used for many games.

Camera supplies. Many advertising brochures and pictures are of interest to students.

Candle and soap shops. Broken candles and damaged soap are good items for the classroom store.

Carpet and rug dealers. Because scraps of carpet can be stitched together for the clubhouse or other special areas in the classroom, they sell extremely well.

Churches. Perhaps the best potential source of reinforcers is the local church. Women's clubs can make beanbags, dolls, stuffed animals, knitted hats and slippers, as well as small arts and crafts items. A Sunday bake sale may donate its proceeds for buying models, trinkets, toiletries, and the like. If the teacher will document the students' improvement and thus demonstrate the effectiveness of the currency-based token economy, churches will often be eager to follow up any initial action with more generosity. Local fraternal organizations fall in a similar category.

Commercial artists. Artists are often willing to give away brushes, paint, or canvas that do not meet their high standards. These items seem to have strong appeal, not only because of their practical value, but because an artist once used them.

Commercial photographers. A commercial photographer does not use every picture he takes. He may be willing to give you some of his unsatisfactory photographs to use as reinforcers.

Dealers in acoustical tile. Scraps of acoustical tile can be used to make bulletin boards. A price can then be assigned to the bulletin boards.

Dealers in agricultural equipment. Calendars showing a picture of a combine or other farm equipment are big sellers.

Dentists. Children's toothbrushes, sample toothpaste, dental floss, and booklets on tooth care are usually available from dentists.

Drapery and curtain retailers. Scraps of materials are reinforcing for some children.

Drive-in restaurants. Many drive-ins feature a special cup or glass for soft drinks, as well as packets of sugar, salt, ketchup, and so forth.

Dry cleaners. Coat hangers have many potential uses. Also, many dry cleaners use advertising gimmicks. We had one particularly good experience with a dry cleaner that used miniature footballs with the name of the business printed on them.

Electric motor repair shops. Old motors are especially appealing to students. However, the teacher must make certain they are safe.

Electricians. Electrical wire can be used to weave rings and bracelets or make stick figures.

Fabric shops. Many times, scraps of fabric are available. These scraps are ideal for making quilts or doll clothes. Old pattern books are sometimes available.

Fire departments. Old water hoses and "Smokey the Bear" items are frequently available.

Fish markets. Large pictures of fish are sometimes available.

Florists. Old pieces of Styrofoam, scraps of colored tinfoil, ribbon, flowers, and plants are potential reinforcers.

Food stores that carry novelty or imported items. Advertising posters and labels written in a foreign language appeal to many children.

Foreign car dealers. Pictures advertising last year's models are available.

Funeral homes. Coffin boxes (not coffins) can be used for sliding down hills, making forts, and so forth. Some funeral homes distribute paper fans that children love to buy in hot weather.

Furniture dealers. Boxes can also be obtained from furniture dealers.

Geologists or state geological surveys. Rock samples are occasionally available.

Greenhouses. Chipped or cracked plant pots can be used to plant apple seeds from apple cores.

Hardware or home improvement stores. Such stores frequently offer free yardsticks.

Heavy hauling equipment dealers. Calendars and pictures are usually available.

Hydraulic equipment dealers. Old pumps are sometimes available. Many boys love to take the pump apart and see how it works.

Industrial developers. Aerial photographs of industrial developments are sometimes available.

Insurance companies. Insurance companies usually have bumper stickers that can be put on bikes, plus advertising gimmicks such as yearly calendars.

Interior decorators. Interior decorators use workups with drawings and the like which are often thrown away.

Jewelers. Old watch and ring boxes are hot items in the classroom store.

Junkyards or dumps. If you have ever watched a child at the dump, you know almost everything is worth bringing home.

Key shops and locksmiths. Old keys, key blanks, and especially locks have an intrinsic appeal all their own.

Knitting shops. If knitting and embroidering are taught in the shop, you may be able to obtain scraps of yarn and embroidery thread, old embroidery hoops, knitting and embroidery needles, and scraps of needlepoint. Boys as well as girls enjoy these items.

Landscape contractors. Sketches and workups for landscapes are available after a job is finished.

Local and long-distance movers. These companies usually have calendars showing the fleet of trucks.

Logging companies. Pictures of logging operations and equipment are good items.

Lumberyards. Lumberyards usually have a scrap box containing wood for kindling. These scraps of wood can be ideal geometric figures for abstract art projects. The scraps can be sold by the store, and the student can be reinforced for making something with them.

Mechanical engineers. Old designs of tools or machinery are often reinforcing.

Marine equipment and supplies. Pictures of sailboats, tugboats, fireboats, and barges.

Mobile home and camper dealers. Some students love to plan future camping trips. When given the opportunity to plan the ideal dream trip, their interest in advertising pictures of campers and camping equipment increases dramatically.

Motorcycle shops. Advertising pictures of the various models are always appealing, but pictures of choppers are valued most highly.

Movie theaters. Pictures of movie stars are sometimes available, and students value these pictures highly.

Newspaper publishers. Newspapers are printed from large rolls of paper. When the end of the roll is near, a new roll is positioned. It is possible to get the ends of these rolls, which contain much usable paper for drawing and so on.

Outboard motor dealers. Advertising pictures of various models are appealing to many students.

Paint stores. Some paint stores will donate painters' hats, stirring sticks, and free samples of paint.

Paperhangers. Scraps of wallpaper have many uses, and the classroom store stands to profit from each.

Physicians. Pamphlets about health care and tongue depressors are potential reinforcers. Tongue depressors can be used to make things such as boats or planes.

Piano dealers. Broken piano strings and keys can be used in art projects. A student can make his own musical instrument with broken strings.

Plastering contractors. Scraps of plasterboard can be used for many art projects; they also make an ideal building material for the neighborhood clubhouse.

Radio stations. Autographed pictures of disc jockeys and old discs can be available

Railroad stations and freight offices. Calendars, advertising pictures, and sometimes old railroad spikes can be obtained.

Realtors. The classroom realtor may need "For Sale" and "Sold" signs, which should be obtained from the classroom store, not from people's houses or lawns.

Resorts. Students often want scenic advertising pictures to decorate their desks.

Roofers. Many students use scraps of tarpaper or shingles in their forts or neighborhood clubhouses.

Seed and bulb wholesalers. Free samples are the best possibility. The seeds and bulbs can be planted in a classroom plot, and produce and flowers can be purchased for the classroom store at wholesale prices and later retailed to students.

Service stations. Most major service stations employ some advertising gimmick to attract customers. In addition to advertising merchandise, old inner tubes, tires, and auto parts are good items for a store. Although the teacher may not particularly want these items, the classroom store most certainly will.

Sheet metal shops. Scraps of sheet metal can be used to make many novel items. If tin snips are used to fashion an animal, we recommend a pair of pliers and a hammer be used to bend over and pound out the sharp edges. The sheet metal could be sold; the hammer and pliers rented.

Sporting goods shop. Advertising for sporting goods shows pictures of professional athletes at their best. These pictures make good items for the store.

Spring steel distributors. Springs of any kind are always big sellers.

Supermarkets. Old advertising offers a wealth of potential for the classroom store. One case in point: at Thanksgiving time, one of the local supermarkets donated a life-size stand-up cardboard pilgrim. This item was greatly desired and sold for a high price at the classroom store.

Travel agencies. Many travel pictures and brochures make ideal additions.

Truck dealers. Advertising pictures of makes and models, from the smallest pickup to the largest tractor-trailer.

TV repair shops. Many potentially useful items can be acquired here; for example, old television sets that still work. One such television set was awarded to the student who made the most overall improvement in reading for the year.

Upholsterers. Scraps of cloth and foam rubber can be sold by the classroom store for making stuffed animals and the like. In fact, the students should obtain most of the materials they need for art projects from the classroom store.

Well drillers. Worn-out drill bits are great potential reinforcers.

Welders. Welding rods can be fashioned into abstract designs.

The fate of the currency-based token economy will be affected to a great extent by the items selected for the store. If a child cannot find something appealing, motivation to work in the classroom may diminish. A good store will therefore contain a wide variety of free or inexpensive items, in-school rentals, and fees for special events and activities.

Some fortunate individuals may teach in a school system that will allocate funds for your economy, or you may have obtained money from a civic-minded organization in your community, perhaps even received some type of grant. With such assistance, you will be able to purchase inexpensive materials to stock the store and supplement them with free items.

Go online and search novelty and carnival supply stores for an array of interesting inexpensive items. You may be surprised at the scope of choices and how inexpensive things are when purchased in bulk.

Rentals can also be used to enhance the selection in your store. For instance, charge a fee to listen (with earphones) to a favorite song, or buy time to work on a jigsaw puzzle placed in the back of the room, or time to color or paint.

One way to acquire reinforcers at no cost is to have a "junk-day auction" of discarded items that children bring from home. For this activity, have the students bring notes from home, stating the parents consider these items to be junk and that the student has permission to auction them. A similar activity is a bake sale. (Again, the student should bring a note from home before an item is auctioned.) Some teachers have found it interesting to introduce a silent auction procedure.

Auctions are exciting to most children. Also, auctions have educational value because the student must:

1. count his money;
2. know how much money he has;
3. know what he wants to buy;
4. realize how much he can afford to spend;
5. know when the bid is higher than the amount of money he has;
6. realize that although he has some money and would like an item, he may be outbid; and
7. understand that when he wins a bid, it is a matter of "cash on the barrelhead."

Students soon learn to listen carefully to the auctioneer and to avoid bidding against themselves.

In addition to its educational value and the excitement it can create in your class, an auction has several other advantages. "Once-in-a-lifetime" items can be offered for sale to all, rather than to the first person who happens upon it on the shelf. Announcing in advance that a football helmet or baseball glove will be auctioned off virtually guarantees an increase in work output among the students; children often beg to stay in from recess to earn more money before the bidding starts. Auctions also reinforce the concept of banking money to save for something special.

Another possibility is to charge admission fees for special events and activities, such as movies, magic shows, field trips, and nature walks around the school. Special events build enthusiasm. When priced right, they can be turned into learning how to save money. Rolls of paper tickets (similar to those issued at raffles) may be economically available at a local discount store.

Once the store has been stocked, prices must be set. Keep in mind that higher prices enable the teacher to reinforce more often and more generously.

A more precise means to determine the cost of an item is to use the formula stated in Chapter 4 regarding question 19, pages 34–45 in the section "Answers to Commonly Asked Questions." Using a currency-based economy, where a dollar equals a token, the formula converts as follows: the number of dollars to charge per penny is determined by the number of children in the class times the number of dollars to be dispensed per child per day times the school days per week, with the result divided by the amount of money (in cents) that the teacher has available to spend in one week. The following example illustrates how this formula works:

A teacher with a class of 30 students wishes to implement a currency economy by dispensing $50 to each child every day. The economy will be in force for the entire week and must be supported from a weekly budget of $3. Using the formula

$$\frac{30 \times 50 \times 5}{300} = 25$$

the teacher determines that she must charge $25 per penny cost of the items in the store. Therefore, a smile ring costing two cents would be worth $50 in the store, a five-cent rubber knife would be worth $125, and a ten-cent after-dinner mint would be worth $250.

Another, more general, method of determining the cost of items may be more appropriate if the store contains many free items and activities. Responsible members of the economy—i.e., the students—act as consultants and suggest what they consider to be fair prices and which items they consider of greater value. With this approach, it will be easy to determine which items are big sellers and which attract little attention. With either method of pricing, it is wise to have bargain sales on items that are not moving and to raise the prices on popular ones.

Store Arrangement and Display

The physical setup of the store and the way items are displayed greatly enhances the realistic atmosphere the currency economy seeks to project. A closet with shelves in it makes a convenient store because the door can be closed when the store is not open for business. Desks or tables can be used as counters. If a closet is unavailable, a table fitted with casters may be the next best thing, since it can be rolled out of sight when the store is closed. A clear plastic cover is useful for keeping eager customers from handling the merchandise.

For students who are adjusting to their first buying experience, items are best arranged according to price. In this way, children will know that items on a particular shelf are beyond their means, that they must concentrate on the items they can afford. Distinctly marked price tags help children who are in the process of learning their numbers. The entire store experience will become a lesson in number concepts as the child begins to see the relationship between numbers and purchasing power.

Staffing the Store

The store can be operated by a single classroom or jointly by several classrooms. In the latter case, the store's potential for expanding its function and providing fresh experiences for the students is greatly increased. Obviously, the teacher will have to adapt suggestions about operating the store according to the resources available. The student-run store can help the teacher who lacks assistance handle this aspect of the economy without any great difficulty.

A likely beginning point in the operation of the store is for an aide to run it, while the teacher continues to work with the children. If no aides or volunteers are available, other children in the school may be the best source of storekeepers as well as store managers. Children with good concepts of numbers and of money exchange should be able to take over without too much guidance. In schools where the economy has existed for several years, older students will already be trained to take over the operation.

Whether volunteers are available or not, the purpose of the currency economy is to involve students as quickly as possible. In addition to easing the teacher's burden, the primary advantage of involving students is career education, at least in a preliminary sense. Here, we refer to career education as an opportunity to learn a variety of skills related to running a store, as well as an appreciation for what it is like to hold a responsible position and earn a salary.

Hiring storekeepers will enable the teacher to capitalize on several realistic aspects of our world. This training applies not only to older students, but to **all** students. Storekeepers and bank tellers have been successfully recruited and trained from second grade on up.

The first step in any hiring procedure is the job application. Figure 7.1 below presents an example of an application form used with second graders. Remember that all these procedures are learning experiences and can be built into the curriculum as units involving arithmetic, reading, and social studies. The application form provides a vehicle for introducing several new concepts to the child. Each child is given a social security card, which can be photocopied (see Figure 7.2). Beginning lessons on the purpose and function of social security would tie in well at this point. A second concept that will be new to children is the request for references, which they will encounter on the application. Again, the goals of career education can be enhanced when you explain the function of references and supplement your explanation by giving each child an opportunity to choose references from among their friends. Practice at writing reference letters and filling out application forms gives the children an opportunity to experience the characteristics that employers consider important. A sample reference letter form is shown in Figure 7.3. The additional concepts of bonding and the power of a signature can also be explained.

The second step in the hiring procedure is the interview. The purpose of the interview is twofold: it allows the teacher or store manager to assess the child's skills related to money, and it gives the child an opportunity to learn what will be expected of him if he gets the job. Figure 7.4 below illustrates some components of a typical interview for the job of storekeeper.

After the applications and interviews are completed, the hiring is done by either the teacher or the store manager.

JOB APPLICATION FORM

Position Applied for:_____   Full time ☐

Part time ☐

Name (print) _____

Address _____

City & state _____

Homeroom teacher _____

Date of birth _____

Reading teacher _____

Math teacher _____

Weight _____ Height _____

Jobs you have been responsible for...

at whome _____

at school _____

in community (church, etc.) _____

Social security number _____

How many days have you been absent from school this year? _____

Member of any clubs or organizations _____

_____

Lists of hobbies & interests _____

_____

References (no relatives) (people who know you well)

1. _____ 2. _____

Parents _____

Brothers and Sisters 1. _____ Age _____

2. _____ Age _____

3. _____ Age _____

4. _____ Age _____

5. _____ Age _____

If employed, when can you start work? _____

Comments:

By signing this application, I promise that all the above statements are true.

Your signature _____

Figure 7–1.

Figure 7–2. Social Security Card. Note: The numbering system indicates the school's identification number, the homeroom number, and the child's own identification number. Copyright © Depositphotos/ginosphotos1.

Since training of the storekeepers will be an essential part of the store's operation, do not assume that only the smartest applicants should be hired. It is quite likely that students who are experiencing difficulty in math may be motivated to learn quickly when presented with numbers from this new angle and will profit most from their employment.

REFERENCE FORM

Dear _____,
Please give your rating of _____ on the following items.

Thank you,
The Garland Rhodes Store

<u>Items</u>

	High	Middle	Low	Unknown
Honesty				
Accepting Responsibility				
Neatness				
Punctuality				
Courtesy				
General Health				
Friendliness				
Appearance				
Leadership Ability				
Math Skills				

Would you recommend this person for the job of:

Store clerk	yes	no
Teller	yes	no
Guard	yes	no
Store manager	yes	no
Bank manager	yes	no

Other comments:

Figure 7–3.

PREPARATION:

Have available various denominations of money, several store items, price tags, and the student's application form. Make notes on the back of the form.

1. Ask the student to identify a variety of bills.
2. Ask him to count a variety of denomination combinations.
3. Ask him to make change for store items.
4. If he has difficulty performing 1, 2, or 3, demonstrate how to do them.
5. Does the student seem to understand these demonstrations?
6. Explain the kinds of things that are important for a storekeeper to be able to do and ask the student whether he believes he can do them.
    a. Count and handle money.
    b. Know how much items cost.
    c. Make change.
    d. Be courteous to customers.
    e. Be neat.
    f. Be punctual.
    g. Be honest and responsible.
    h. Communicate.
7. Fill in any parts missing on application.
8. Answer any questions the student may have about the job.

Figure 7–4. Components of an Interview for Employment in the Store.

When training students for work in the store, you can begin by concentrating on recognition of different dollar denominations, how to make change, and keep simple records. A more complex program, however, can include training in customer relations—i.e., courtesy, friendliness, and cooperation; how to price items and display them attractively; and how to organize special sales. A trip to a local store would be a worthwhile experience at this time. Here, students can observe the way shelves are stocked, cash registers are operated, and sales are advertised. Classroom units on stores and selling would be natural outgrowths of this experience.

When storekeepers are being trained to assume their jobs, you can make provisions to increase their experiential learning in several ways. A time clock or sign-in sheet (see Figure 7.5) not only emphasizes the importance of being on time for work, but gives the teacher an opportunity to introduce the concept of being docked if and when necessary. Schedules can be posted so that workers can see when they are expected to work. Salaries will expose the children to the idea of dollars per hour, and graded pay scales can be set up according to time on the job and the importance of a particular job in the store's hierarchy. As in every other aspect of the currency economy, the employment of students in the store is an open-ended suggestion that can be carried as far as the teacher desires.

Employee _____

Date	In	Out	Time Worked

Total Time Worked _____
Approved _____

Figure 7–5. Sign-in Sheet for Store Employees.

GOING TO THE STORE

Although staffing the store offers many opportunities for teaching skills, most children's experiences with the store will come through personal visits. Chapter 5 suggests that trips to the store should occur frequently at the beginning while the children are adjusting to the new system and before they have learned to delay gratification. Within a couple of weeks, visits can gradually be decreased to once a week. At this point, disruption of class activities should be minimal.

Visiting the store is likely to be a highlight of the day for the children, so make certain that all of them attend an equal amount of times. The storekeeper can keep simple records of all customers, and the list can then be checked against the class rolls. If an aide or trained student is running the store, several children can go to the store while others continue with their class-work. This arrangement frees the teacher from involvement in the entire store procedure. In addition to recording each child's attendance, it will be useful for the storekeeper to record the amount of money spent by each customer. The teacher will then have a list that can be checked to ensure that a particular child has received sufficient payments (reinforcements). This list may also be helpful in the event of a stealing epidemic.

A trip to the store should be an educational experience. Many children, especially younger ones, may count poorly and have problems identifying different denominations of money. Thus, it might be a good idea to have students who can count well assist these children during store visits. Each child should have the opportunity to count his own money and receive help only if he needs it. Also, each child should have the freedom to choose the item he wants. The storekeeper can facilitate the learning process by asking customers how much money they have and directing them to the shelves that contain the merchandise they can afford. It is also advantageous if the customers can make their purchases one by one and count out the correct amount of money to pay each bill.

The operating procedures outlined have been used successfully with children who are only seven or eight years old. By modifying these basic procedures, teachers have been able to use them in both individual classrooms and in cooperative ventures among three rooms with a centrally located store. The store can provide additional learning experiences by incorporating a sales tax, mail-order buying, installment plans, and by running classified ads or store sale ads in the school newspaper.

CREDIT CARDS

In individual classrooms, the use of credit cards is not very feasible because of the amount of time it takes to design and execute one properly. However, if several classes or an entire school adopt a currency-based economy, a credit system may prove to be a boon. The first report of setting up a credit card system was circulated in 1970 by Paul Lehrer. Teachers who are interested in knowing more about the use of a credit card system may want to review his classic work, "The Use of a Credit Card in a Token Economy," *Journal of Applied Behavioral Analysis*, vol. 3, 1970. In addition to a description of how the credit card system was implemented, this article also contains illustrations of a credit card slip and a credit statement, information about obtaining credit cards, and cost estimates for embossing.

Although the store is an integral part of the currency economy and provides many opportunities for learning, the concept of banking broadens the instructional value of the currency-based token system.

CHAPTER 8

Banking

Establishing a classroom bank within the currency-based token economy affords a relevant education and an advanced curriculum for the children. The bank offers the children experiences that many would not normally encounter until much later in life. It helps them understand the economic and social currents at work in their world today.

Setting up the Bank

The bank does not demand as much space as the store. It can consist of a desk or two where the tellers can sit and serve fellow students. To add a special touch, obtain a cardboard refrigerator carton from an appliance store and cut a window in it. The bank's appearance may be a factor in generating student interest in saving money, especially with young children.

Preparation of materials for opening the bank will not be too demanding. Necessary items will include a savings passbook for each child (Figure 8.1) and a record-keeping system for the tellers. A loose-leaf notebook with one page per child or a box containing index cards will serve this purpose well. Figure 8.2 shows a simple record sheet for bank transactions.

Introducing Banking

Unlike the store, familiar to all children, the bank may be completely foreign to many. The bank's success will depend on orientation the teacher provides in advance of opening day.

Local resources should not be overlooked in planning the banking unit. Bankers are usually honored when asked to come to school and discuss the way their bank operates. Once the children understand the basics, they will be ready for a visit to the bank. The vault is guaranteed to interest children not previously exposed to banks.

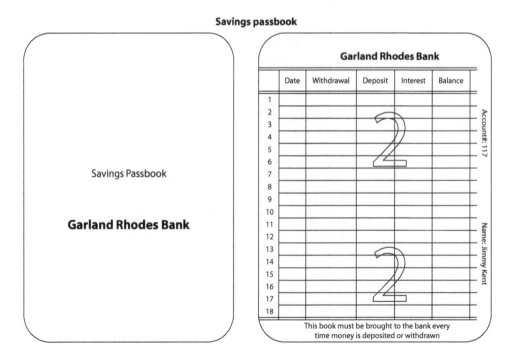

Figure 8–1. Savings Passbook

Name _____ Class _____

Account # _____

Date	Deposit	Withdrawal	Interest

Figure 8–2. Record Sheet for Daily Bank Transactions

Staffing the Bank

After experiencing a bank's operations, interested students will be ready to apply for work in their "local" bank. The application form in Figure 7.1 can be used to begin the hiring procedures for the tellers. The follow-up interview can be altered somewhat to reflect the different skill requirements the job demands. (Figure 8.3 illustrates some possible components of the interview.)

Interviewing, selecting, and training tellers can be facilitated by using older students, who will rapidly learn what competencies the teacher is interested in achieving. In addition to abilities related to adding and subtracting money, several banking skills may have to be incorporated into the training program. Customer relations should be explained to the tellers so they develop a friendly, cordial manner while carrying out their duties. Tellers must be able to follow banking routines such as locating the customer's number and file card, entering deposits or withdrawals, and returning the passbook to the student, as well as making change and computing interest.

The bank can be run in a manner similar to the store with respect to the employees. Salaries can be set that reflect time, work experience, and the level of the job in the banking hierarchy. Initially, the bank manager may be an older student or an aide, but eventually he should

PREPARATION:

Have the following available: bills of several denominations, addition and subtraction problems, the bank passbook, and each student's application form. Record answers on the back of the form.

1. Ask the student to count by 5s, 10s, 20s, and 50s and combinations of these denominations.
2. Have the student exchange large bills for small ones and vice versa.
3. Demonstrate how to do steps 1 and 2 if the student cannot perform it on his own.
4. Assess the student's ability to learn these tasks after they are demonstrated.
5. Ask the student to read and write different amounts of money.
6. Ask the student to add and subtract one-, two-, and three-digit numbers.
7. Discuss the important aspects of a teller's job:
   a. Counting and handling money.
   b. Exchanging large and small bills.
   c. Addition and subtraction.
   d. Ability to read and write numbers and money words.
   e. Neatness, courtesy, and punctuality.
   f. Responsibility and honesty.
8. Fill in an y blanks on the application form.
9. Answer any questions the student may have about the position.

Figure 8–3. Components of an Interview for Employment in the Bank

be found from among the bank employees in the class. The manager will be responsible for scheduling, handling payday, and overseeing the daily running of the bank.

Going to the Bank

Before the bank is opened, students have probably been storing their money in their desks between trips to the store. Complaints about lost or stolen money can be capitalized on to encourage saving via a savings passbook. Earning interest is another good way to entice children to use the bank's services. Initially, all members of the class should have a chance to visit the bank and make their transactions. After this initial opportunity, visits to the bank should be frequent enough for even the thriftiest student. By the time the bank opens, each student should understand all bank terms. Someone could review these terms with students from time to time or when deemed necessary. In subsequent visits, the student should be aware of their balance before withdrawing or depositing money.

Earning interest generates its own "interest" in the children. Teach them to understand the concept clearly and what it means in terms of hard cash. By computing their interest once a week, the students can watch their money grow. An interest rate of 10 percent will simplify the teller's calculations and represent a visible addition to most balances.

A checking account will be especially valuable for the older child who may already be familiar with savings operations. Although checking accounts necessitate additional classroom instruction, the time is well invested because of their relevance to the real world. As with savings, materials are easily accessible to develop a unit on writing checks and balancing checkbooks. The introduction of checking will require the printing of checks, further training for tellers or the addition of another teller, and a method of controlling the flow of bad checks. Checks can easily be run off on a photocopy machine (see Figure 8.4).

A third service a bank can offer without any special difficulty is the use of safe deposit boxes. Children interested in this service can bring a shoe box from home and pay a small monthly rental fee. Teachers can stress the privacy to which all boxholders are entitled. Provisions should be made for the boxes to be kept in a private place. A cardboard refrigerator carton would provide a private place for the child to handle his secret business. The teacher's assurance that boxes will not be checked encourages the students to take advantage of the service. In keeping with this promise, we know that the safety deposit boxes have been a popular facet of the bank's operation. Some young children use safe deposit more than any other banking service.

A fourth option of the classroom bank is granting loans. Loans present the children with the other side of interest—how it can work against them. An educational unit on loans can stress the advantages and pitfalls involved in borrowing money. Working a loan service into the class bank would probably entail the training of a loan officer (perhaps the bank manager), a discussion of a good credit reference, and the importance of paying bills on time.

Policy and Decision Committee

A policy and decision committee can supervise the bank operation as well as the store. It can handle complaints and suggestions from the class about how things are being run. An idea-and-gripe box accessible to students provides the committee with issues to be dealt with. Given responsibility, the committee members are likely to treat each comment fairly and adopt those ideas that will increase efficiency and service. A second major function of the committee is to

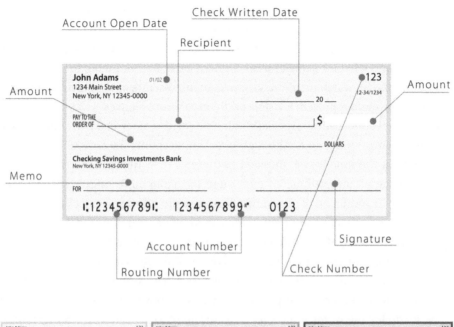

Figure 8–4. Sample Check. <u>Note:</u> This numbering system follows that of the social security system as mentioned on Figure 7.2. Copyright © Depositphotos/ cteconsulting.

serve as a judiciary council for violations within the system such as stealing. Procedures for implementing committee recommendations could include weekly meetings and subsequent reports to the constituents.

Establishing the committee provides an opportunity to bring the electoral process into the curriculum. One elaborate economy became involved in campaigns with posters, speeches, and voting by secret ballot. This is an example of the economy working for the teacher, allowing curriculum topics—normally only read about and discussed—to be experienced.

Guards

Employing guards to protect the bank and store promotes self-discipline among the children. The guards' primary role is to prevent running, disruptive loud talking, and hassling in general. Awarded and displaying a badge, the guard is empowered to evict the disruptive student from the activity. In addition, the guard should handle all transactions involving safe deposit boxes. If running to the bank or store becomes a chronic problem, the guard can issue tickets to the offenders.

Establishing a bank in the currency economy is an excellent complement to other educational facets of the system. Banking can not only be educational, but also exciting.

Get Ready and Go

As indicated before, we strongly recommend that anyone attempting to establish a currency system adopt the following bywords: *preparation* and *organization*. It is impossible to reap the full educational benefits of the currency system while flying by the seat of your pants. Having established a number of currency economies, we are convinced that poor preparation and lack of organization will doom the system.

If, when setting up a currency system, the teacher relies on her intuition to determine what should be done, she will undoubtedly encounter many complications, become frustrated, and give up. As with any tool, if this happens, it is not the fault of the tool, but rather the worker: a good carpenter never blames his tools. The currency system is a tool with vast potential. If it is well planned and organized, its potential can be realized.

Setting up the Economy

There are six sequential steps involved in using currency in the classroom:

1.   Making the money;
2.   Planning activities;
3.   Preparing materials;
4.   Paying students for work completed;
5.   Giving students an opportunity to spend the money;
6.   Evaluating student progress.

The amount of time and energy devoted to each step depends on the students' ability levels and the extent to which the economy is used. The remainder of this chapter contains detailed, explicit directions that any teacher can follow to establish a currency system with a minimum of time and effort.

STEP 1. MAKING THE MONEY

A currency-based token economy uses paper money, which is artificial **only** in the sense it cannot be exchanged in the adult world. In the micro society of the classroom, it is as real as life itself.

Paper money rather than coin is used exclusively in a currency-based token economy because it has the following advantages:

1.   It is inexpensive to produce.
2.   It is easily made from available materials.
3.   It can be conveniently carried and stored.
4.   It reduces noise pollution.
5.   It can be produced in a variety of denominations.

We suggest the teacher start with one ream of 8 ½" × 11" paper, preferably green. Draw six bills per sheet (see Figure 9.1). On each bill, include a picture of some kind; the number of denomination (e.g., $20), the name of the denomination (e.g., Twenty Dollars); and the name of the currency (e.g., Central Elementary Currency). To avoid legal complications, the words *No Value* and *Not Negotiable* should be placed in a conspicuous place. (It would be wise to explain the reason for these words to the students).

Recommended dimensions of currency

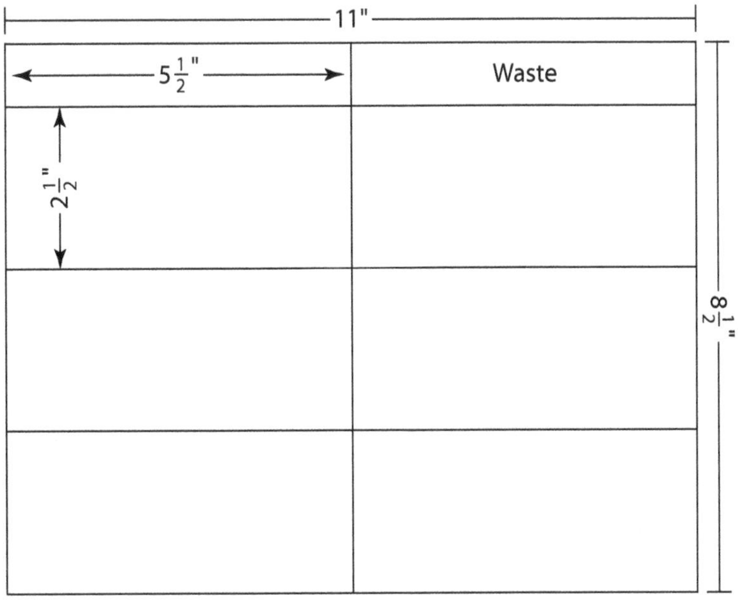

Figure 9–1. Recommended Dimensions of Currency.

For first runs, print on one side only. Later, more elaborate types of printing and graphics may be desired. The bulk of bills should be $1, with very few denominations of $5 and $10. As the currency system takes hold, the denominations of $20, $50, and $100 may be added.

STEP 2. PLANNING AND ACTIVITIES

Using the currency is a new and exciting experience for students. As with any novel item or approach, the children's initial enthusiasm will be high. The key to planning activities is to capitalize on and build that enthusiasm. Students will be eager to explore new avenues of learning, but be prepared: you must know in advance precisely what you want students to do to earn money and how their initiative will be rewarded.

STEP 3. PREPARING THE MATERIALS

The students'eagerness to work will generate a need for many more materials than usual; the supply of instructional materials must meet the demand. If the supply of materials lags behind demand, the students will lose their enthusiasm for the work. The instructional materials should be well organized and easy to use.

The students' impatient desire to work can also cause the teacher to abuse the system inadvertently. Currency reinforcers can be misused if the teacher has children churn out dozens of worksheets solely to keep busy. To avoid this situation, the teacher must constantly evaluate whether the exercises assigned are appropriate.

STEP 4. PAYING THE STUDENTS FOR WORK COMPLETED

Work should be reinforced (paid off) only after it has been completed according to the criterion. The students' work should be corrected and paid off as quickly and efficiently as possible. If the time lag between completion and the correction and payoff is too long, a logjam, so to speak, will be created. Any such logjam will dampen the students' enthusiasm. It will necessitate recording what has been promised and what is past due. Students are extremely sensitive to any violation of the teacher's promise to pay. Pay workers quickly, accurately, and fairly for all their satisfactory work.

STEP 5. GIVE THE STUDENTS AN OPPORTUNITY TO SPEND THE MONEY

Chapter 7 explains how to set up the store and how to secure goods and services. Items in the store must be priced appropriately and marked. A wide variety of goods and services is required because of individual differences among the students. Keep the store supplied with reinforcers. A record of stock and sales will indicate which items are most in demand and which items generate no interest. Any delay in supplying popular items will undermine the operation and, as a consequence, adversely affect the currency system. Furthermore, keep in mind the students' levels of readiness. For example, if students cannot count to 20, it is unwise to price items at that level. Because opportunities to go to the store must be relatively frequent, you must have a well-stocked store with adequate business hours.

STEP 6. EVALUATING THE STUDENTS' PROGRESS

This aspect of the program is very important. Because student progress is directly affected by the currency system, any evaluation of the students evaluates the currency indirectly. Therefore, to assess the students' progress accurately, collect sufficient preliminary data. If your findings are favorable to the economy, there is no problem. But if the data reflects no change, you should consider alternative ways of using the economy. If the alternatives produce no change, then the system should be discarded.

Establishing the Currency System

The following examples illustrate the simplest way to establish the currency system in a class-room. These procedures are merely a way to start, not the terminal goal. To illustrate subject diversity and developmental level in relation to the initial activities, examples are provided for second-grade math, fourth-grade reading, and sixth-grade social studies. Only three examples are provided. Modify the specific example to fit your own situation. To present the three examples of step-by-step procedures, some repetition is inevitable. Note that in each of the following examples, no effort is made to begin with a daylong program. Unless a teacher is extremely competent, organized, and well prepared, has a lot of help, is physically strong and emotionally stable, an attempt to implement the currency system on a full-day basis immediately would be imprudent. The daylong program should come later after an initial period of adjustment.

EXAMPLE 1: SECOND-GRADE MATH

This example assumes the math period lasts approximately 60 minutes and includes 30 students. Although not essential, it will help to have the assistance of a teacher's aide.

FIRST DAY

Making and using the money. The money should already be made. Use only $1 bills the first day, and plan to pay each student at least $25. You should have **at least** 50 times as many bills as you have students before you begin.

Planning the activities. Since the money must be introduced to the children on the first day, it would be wise to use the first 30 minutes to present the money, the store, and the way children can earn and spend. When they give you their full attention, reward them with a $1 bill. Learn to teach while distributing the money. If you stop talking until the money has been distributed to each child, you will lose too much time to make the use of money practical.

Two things will occur on the first day: you and your aide will be exhausted, and you both will be amazed that you personally and positively contacted the students as many times as you did. Try to reward all the students at least five times during this 30-minute period. For the next 15 minutes, give all the students a worksheet with 20 easy problems on it. Tell the students that for each problem they solve correctly, you will pay them $1. Every student should get every problem right. Each now has $25. During the last 15 minutes, open the store and let the students spend their money. Most of the items in the store should cost about $25. Because time is limited (about 30 seconds per student), tell them not to dawdle when deciding what to buy. Since some students will go to the store before others, they will have time on their hands. Plan to have supplementary work and activities for which they will be paid.

It should be emphasized that the money belongs to the students and that if they have not spent all of it by the end of the day, they are still responsible for it. You may wish to provide the students with an envelope in which to keep their money. Explain to them that if they count or play with the money at an inappropriate time (i.e., other than math class), it may be taken away.

Preparing the materials. Prepare a worksheet with 20 problems that every student can complete correctly in 15 minutes. At the end of this period, the children will be going to the store with a dollar for each correct problem. As they rotate to the store, provide those not at the store with a supplementary activity. This could include additional worksheets, workbook pages, problems on the board, or math games and puzzles. Hopefully, the work can combine the dual purposes of providing appropriate work for the students while giving them another chance to work the system. Naturally, the activities will afford the children an additional opportunity to earn dollars.

Paying the students for work completed. This is probably the most difficult phase of the entire program. The shortest possible delay between completion of task, correction, and payoff can be accomplished only if the teacher is well organized. We have found that a stand-up flag (see Figure 9.2 below) is effective. When the student's work is ready to be corrected, he simply takes the flag out of his desk and stands it on the top of his desk. The teacher and aide move from flag to flag, correcting papers. Students should raise their hands only when they want to ask questions or request help. A large amount of individualized instruction takes place at the time the papers are being corrected. When paying the student, ask him to count the money he receives.

Giving the students an opportunity to spend the money. The time spent at the store is initially extremely important.

We have suggested 15 minutes during a 60-minute period because the store can be operated in that time. However, if you can spare more time, we highly recommend that you do so. Acutally, it would be preferable to extend the math period so that everyone has an opportunity to browse before buying. Remember that if the student does not have an adequate opportunity to spend his money, the money is worthless. We also recommend that the aide operate the store initially; this will leave you free to assist students with supplementary work or activities.

Stand-up flag for signaling
teacher to correct papers

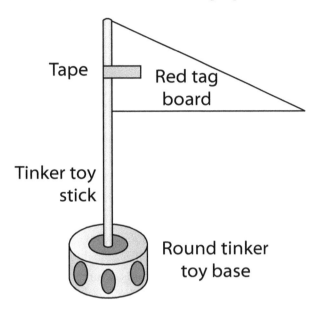

Figure 9–2. Stand-up Flag for Signaling Teacher to Correct Papers.

Purchased By	Item	Cost	Date
1. Jim Smith	Yo-yo	$42	2/29
2. Susie Tanna	Gum	$12	3/1
3. Sam Abbey	Frisbee	$64	3/1
4. Kim Payne	Jacks	$31	3/2
5. Janet Lou	Candy	$15	3/2
6. Louie Burke	Ring	$64	3/2
7. Mary Burn	Smiley-face Sticker	$5	3/3
8. Jim Smith	Yo-yo	$42	3/3
9. Carol Lynn	Plant	$45	3/3
10. James Shears	Book	$18	3/4
11.			
12.			
13.			

Figure 9–3. Sheet for Purchase of Goods from Store.

Beginning on the first day, the aide should keep a record of items purchased at the store. (For a sample record sheet, see Figure 9.3.) The record sheet is used to note the popular items and those that are liabilities. As mentioned in Chapter 7, this information will be invaluable in stocking, pricing, and planning future sales.

To increase the learning potential of the store visit, the aide should make certain that each child counts the money he needs out loud, as well as any change given. Although in the confusion of the first day you will be tempted to count it for the slower ones, setting the precedent of having the child responsible will, in the long run, not only reinforce his number skills, but also increase the store's efficiency.

EVALUATING THE STUDENTS' PROGRESS

Before the first day, you should record between five and ten days of data on the quantity and quality of work produced by each student. You may wish to include the number of problems completed, the type and difficulty of the problems, and the number of errors, as well as his neatness. Figure 9.4 is an example of a simple record-keeping instrument. What you are looking for is evidence of whether or not the economy is improving the children's work and work habits.

SECOND DAY

<u>**Making and using the money.**</u> Again, only $1 bills should be used.

<u>**Planning the activities.**</u> Plan to spend about 15 minutes reviewing the use of the money, the store, how the money is earned, and troubleshoot any problems that may have occurred on the first day. During this period, pay each student as often as possible (at least five times), but first make certain that each one earns his money by doing what you want him to do. In the next 15 minutes, plan a large group activity: e.g., learning to carry in addition. In teaching the lesson, offer the children many opportunities to respond to your questions and instructions. When they respond, be sure to reinforce the behaviors you desire. Have a worksheet on which students can write their answers. In that way, you will not fall into the trap of reinforcing only the brightest or most vocal students. If you want all students to be involved, you must reward each one for participating. Prepare the worksheet so that each student can be reinforced at least five times.

During the next 15 minutes, break into small groups. This is an ideal time for you and the aide to individualize your instruction. If possible, divide the class into at least two homogeneous

Name: Johnny Smith				
Date	Type of Problem Behavior	Number of Problems Completed	Number of Errors	Neatness
10–4	3-row, 2-column, no carry addition	10	8	Poor
10–5	Same	10	2	Avg.
10–6	Same	10	10	Good
10–7	3-row, 2-column carry addition	4	3	Poor
10–8	Same	6	1	Avg.
10–11	Same	6	0	Avg.
Continue				

Figure 9–4. Form for Collecting Data on Performance.

groups so you can present <u>appropriate</u> concepts to more than one student at a time. The other groups can do worksheets appropriate to their group level. The aide should be correcting and paying the children as you move from group to group. Each group should have an opportunity to earn at least $5 while you instruct them and $10 for the work they do while you are with other groups. In the last 15 minutes, supplementary games, activities, worksheets, and workbooks should be available to students who are not at the store. The students should receive remuneration commensurate with their ability and the supplementary activity they chose.

Preparing materials. The materials you will need are the group instruction worksheets; small-group instruction and practice worksheets; and supplementary games, activities, workbooks, and the like.

Paying the students for work completed. The procedure is similar to that used on Day One. You may already have caught on to a system, which makes this step easier to administer. If you are having problems, evaluate the system and try to improve it. Constant awareness of procedures will help you administer the program as parsimoniously as possible.

Giving the students an opportunity to spend the money. Since the students are already familiar with the store and its contents, this part of the program should be relatively simple. It would be wise to introduce some higher-priced items so that some of the children may want to start saving their money.

Evaluating student progress. The second day is really the student's first opportunity to be highly productive. Record the quantity and quality of work produced.

THIRD DAY

Making and using the money. Use only $1 bills again today.

Planning the activities. Begin with large-group instruction, and structure it much as you did on Day Two. Small-group instruction can also be structured similarly to Day Two. On the third day, set up an individual file folder for each student, and allow the students 15 minutes to complete the work in the folder. The last 15 minutes should again be devoted to the store, supplementary activities, and so on.

Preparing the materials. By the third day, a pattern should begin to develop. First, worksheets for large-group instruction and practice sheets should be prepared. Second, worksheets for small-group instruction and practice sheets should be prepared. Third, the individual folders are new and should contain work appropriate to each individual student. The worksheets, workbook pages, and so on should be marked at the top with the price you will pay for successful completion of the work (see Figure 10.1 in the next chapter). Fourth, supplementary worksheets, workbooks, games, and the like should be provided.

Paying the students for work completed. A system for payment should definitely be taking hold. If not, ask yourself whether you are spending too much time with each student or whether you are counting the money too slowly. Observations and questions such as these will help you improve your system. The use of the stand-up flags (see Figure 9.2) should be helpful, especially in conjunction with the individual folders.

Giving the students an opportunity to spend the money. Follow the same procedure as in Day One and Day Two.

Evaluating student progress. Continue to record the quality and quantity of work produced. Because the individual folders are corrected at the time they are completed (other students can help you correct them), you should have a good idea about each student's standing and progress. Before making up tomorrow's folder, check whether all the work was completed, how many errors were made, and if the student needed help to finish. These steps will help you determine what to include in tomorrow's folder. The folders give you an invaluable opportunity to individualize your instruction and reach students on a one-to-one basis. Your personal knowledge of each student will increase dramatically with the use of the folders.

FOURTH DAY

Making and using the money. Again, use only $1 bills.

Planning the activities. Continue trying to improve on the previous day's activities.

Preparing the materials. Follow the same procedures as for Day Three.

Paying the students for work completed. Try to make greater use of self-correction procedures and student aides.

Giving the students an opportunity to spend the money. Follow the procedure outlined for Day Three.

Evaluating the student's progress. Follow the procedure outlined for Day Three.

FIFTH DAY

Follow the procedures outlined for the fourth day.

SECOND WEEK

Making and using the money. Introduce $5 bills only to students who thoroughly understand all the concepts involved with $1 bills.

Planning the activities. Refine your techniques. If there are any recurrent problems, seek a more efficient means of conducting this portion of the program.

Preparing the materials. Follow the procedure outlined for the fifth day. The file folders will be the most time consuming. It would be wise to organize your materials so that the material is sequential, run off in advance, and easy to obtain and include in the folders.

Paying the students for work completed. The system of correction and payment should be well organized by now. If not, consider correcting problems on a random basis.

Giving the students an opportunity to spend the money. The operation of the store should be reduced to Monday, Wednesday, and Friday. You should have a good idea of which items are popular and which are not by checking your records of purchases.

Evaluating student progress. Continue to record the quantity and quality of work throughout the second week. At the end of the second week, compare the last ten days with the pre-currency data you collected.

THIRD WEEK

Making and using the money. Introduce $10 bills, $20 bills, and so on to students who are ready.

Planning the activities. Follow the procedure outlined for the second week.

Preparing materials. Follow the procedure outlined for the second week.

Paying the students for work completed. Follow the procedure outlined for the second week.

Allow the students to spend the money. The store should be open on Fridays only, and this schedule should be maintained for the rest of the year. The store should be stocked with many novel and relatively inexpensive items. Establish a bank (see Chapter 8).

Evaluate student progress. You should make a concentrated effort to refine your techniques with any student who is not producing a large amount of high-quality work.

REMAINDER OF THE YEAR

Because the students are now familiar with the currency system, it will be much easier to introduce it into other academic areas. Begin to do so gradually.

EXAMPLE 2: FOURTH-GRADE READING

There are many different approaches to teaching reading. The following example illustrates how to set up a currency system following one approach. If the approach does not completely parallel the one you have been using, do not feel that it is impossible to use the currency. You need to modify the example to fit your situation in order to incorporate the currency-based token economy.

Again, we will assume that the period lasts approximately 60 minutes and includes 30 students. Furthermore, the approach used to teach reading employs large-group instruction, small-group instruction, individualized teaching, and supplementary materials, games, and activities. The help of an aide is beneficial, but not essential.

FIRST DAY

Making and using the money. The money should already be made. Use only $1 bills the first day.

Planning the activities. The store and how money is earned and spent must be introduced the first day. Devote about 30 minutes to this activity. The students should be able to understand what is expected of them and how they can best function under such a system. Allow time for questions. Try to generate enthusiasm. A good way to approach this period is to ask the students for their attention, and when they comply, pay them $1. With an aide's assistance, this task is relatively easy. However, you should become accustomed to paying, talking, and teaching at the same time. If you always wait until you have paid all the students before you continue, too much time will be lost to make the use of money practical. If you have an aide and she pays half the students, the problem of reaching each student should not be too great.

Arrange to reinforce each student at least five times (make certain that before you pay the students, they have earned the money by doing what you want and expect them to do). In the next 15 minutes, present a large-group activity in which each student will earn at least $10. If you want all your students to become involved, you must reward them for participating. The easiest way is to provide a worksheet on which the students can write their answers. In this way, you avoid falling into the trap of rewarding only the brightest and the most vocal students. During the next 15 minutes, divide your class into two or more smaller, homogeneous groups, and make short, small-group presentations in which each student has an opportunity to earn at least $5. The remaining small groups that are working while you are presenting should have worksheets, workbooks, and so forth to use for practice. The aide should be moving from group to group, correcting and paying students for work completed. Each student should receive an additional $5 for the work he has completed. In the last 15 minutes, give the students an opportunity to go to the store. Have supplementary work ready with appropriate payments for those who finish at the store early. If possible, extend the period until all students have had an opportunity to browse and purchase.

Preparing the materials. You will need the following materials for the first day: money; large-group activity answer sheets; small-group activity answer sheets; small-group practice worksheets, workbooks, and the like; supplementary activities, worksheets, games, and materials; and the store (see Chapter 7).

Paying the students for work completed. This is the most difficult phase of the entire operation. It is best to maintain the shortest possible delay between the completion of work and its correction and payoff. A stand-up flag (see Figure 9.2) is extremely helpful. Have the students stand the flag upright on their desk when their work is ready to be corrected. In that way, raising hands can be reserved for questions and requests for assistance; the teacher and aide can move from flag to flag, correcting and paying for work. It is easy to identify students who need assistance. A large amount of individualized instruction can take place while the papers are corrected.

Giving the students an opportunity to spend the money. On the first day, the students should earn about $20. Consequently, a sufficient number of items priced around $30 should be stocked in the store so that every student can spend his money if he wants to. The price range can go as high as you wish, but keep in mind that, initially, most students should have an opportunity to spend their money frequently. If the concept of saving is introduced before the concept of spending is fully understood and enjoyed, you may defeat your purpose. You will, however, have some students who wish to save from the very first day. Be prepared for them with items priced high enough to require saving for several days.

We recommend that the aide operate the store at first, using a record sheet that is similar to the one shown in Figure 9.3. The record sheet will help you identify fast- and slow-selling items. When the aide operates the store, you are free to instruct students, and the opportunities for one-to-one instruction vastly increase.

Evaluating student progress. Before establishing the currency system, you should collect between five and ten days of data on the quantity and quality of work produced. The type of information you collect will depend entirely on the reading approach you are using. Initially, your record keeping will be simplified if you chose only to collect data on only one aspect. For instance, Figure 9.5 illustrates a form that can be used for oral reading. Reading rate per minute and number of errors have been selected to assess improvement. Later, separate evaluation sheets can be developed for silent reading, comprehension skills, word-attack skills, individual reading of library books, and so on.

The first day may not provide you with sufficient evidence to draw any conclusions, but you can record the quantity and quality of work produced for later analysis. The child's increased motivation for success will hopefully result in gains similar to those noted in Figure 9.5.

The relationship between speed and errors is apparent. With this kind of data sheet, the pattern of errors should be discernible (e.g., the student fails to consistently read suffixes).

SECOND DAY

Making and using the money. Continue using $1 bills and introduce $5 bills.

Planning activities. You should only require about five minutes to review the currency system, but take whatever time is necessary to assure a smooth operation. Reward the students at

Oral Reading Name: Johnny Smith		
Date	**Rate per Minute**	**Number of Errors**
10-4	132	6
10-5	129	4
10-6	148	10
10-7	120	2
10-8	115	0

Figure 9–5. Form for Collecting Data on Oral Reading.

least twice during this time. The next 15 minutes can be devoted to large-group instruction, anything from isolated word-attack skills to generating an interest in reading books. Whatever you choose, though, should have the potential for rewarding student participation. An activity sheet for a student's individual answers is recommended. Prepare to have at least $10 worth of answers. If the unit happens to cover comprehension skills, for example, you could (1) introduce the skill; (2) list the steps that help students remember the skill; and (3) include five questions worth $2 each that can be answered on the activity sheet related to the skill.

The next 25 minutes can be devoted to small-group instruction. Budget your time so that you can teach each group. Have the aide correct and pay off students who are doing practice exercises. Follow approximately the same procedure as for Day One. The students should have an opportunity to earn about $5 during small-group instruction and about $15 from the aide in practice activities and drills. Devote the last 15 minutes to operating the store, supplementary work, and activities.

Preparing the materials. The materials needed for the second day are $1 and $5 bills; large-group answer sheets; small-group answer sheets; practice worksheets, workbooks, projects, and the like; and supplementary activities.

Paying the students for work completed. A system should begin to evolve. Be organized in this phase, or the entire program will be jeopardized. Systematically review your procedures to identify more efficient means of operation.

Give the students an opportunity to spend the money. The studetns are already familiar with the store and its operation. Follow the same procedure as in Day One.

Evaluating student progress. Continue to record data on the quality and quantity of work produced; it will be needed for future analysis.

THIRD DAY

Making and using the money. Continue to use $1 and $5 bills. Introduce $10 bills today.

Plan the activities. Use the first 15 minutes for large-group instruction. Follow the procedure outlined for Day Two. In the following 15 minutes, break into your small groups; follow the procedure outlined for Day Two. In the next 15 minutes, individualize your program by introducing a file folder with work that is appropriate to each student's abilities. Plan a reading exercise and workbook or worksheet practice that will be most beneficial to the individual student. This kind of prescriptive teaching is especially valuable in assuring progress (without deficiencies) in sequenced reading competencies. Be certain that each activity offers the student an opportunity to earn as he learns. The recommended payment is $25 for the first 45 minutes. In the last 15 minutes, open the store, and assist the students in supplementary work and activities.

Prepare the materials. The materials needed for Day Three are $1, $5, and $10 bills; large-group activity sheets; small-group activity sheets; small group practice workbooks, worksheets, and the like; and individual folders holding work customized for each student. All work should be priced appropriately.

Pay the students for work completed. If you still have difficulty with this phase, consider checking random problems for correctness. Otherwise, follow the procedure outlined for Day Two.

Give the students an opportunity to spend the money. This portion of the program should be the easiest one. If there are behavioral problems, try rewarding the student who behaves well with a $5 bonus.

Evaluate student progress. One important part of today's evaluation is the individual file folder. If a student seems unable to do the assigned work, now is the time to catch it. Carefully review your expectations and his apparent abilities. Although you should continue to collect data on the quantity and quality of work, it is still too early to make a reliable comparison.

FOURTH DAY

Making and using the money. Continue to use $1, $5, and $10 bills. Introduce the $20 bills to students who are ready.

Plan the activities. Allow 15 minutes for large-group instruction, 15 minutes for small-group instruction and practice, 15 minutes for individualized teaching and work, and 15 minutes for the store and supplementary activities. Follow the procedure outlined for Day Three.

Prepare the materials. Follow the procedure outlined for Day Three.

Pay the students for work completed. Try to make greater use of self-correction procedures and student assistance.

Give the students an opportunity to spend the money. Follow the procedures outlined for Day Three.

Evaluate student progress. Follow the procedures outlined for Day Three.

FIFTH DAY

Introduce the $50 bill, and follow the procedures outlined previously.

SECOND WEEK

Making and using the money. Introduce the $100 bill.

Plan the activities. Refine your techniques. If recurrent problems exist, seek a more efficient means of conducting that portion of the program.

Prepare the materials. Follow the procedure outlined for Day Five. The file folders will be the most time consuming. It is wise to organize your materials so that they are sequenced; run them off in advance, keep them easy to obtain, and include in the file folders.

Pay the students for work completed. The system of correcting and paying should be well organized by now. Evaluate your procedures systematically to see whether you can further refine them. A fairly elaborate student-run bank should be considered (see Chapter 8).

Give the students an opportunity to spend the money. Cut the store hours to Monday, Wednesday, and Friday. Student operation of the store should be considered (see Chapter 7). Decide what items are popular and what items are not popular from the records of purchase.

Evaluate student progress. Continue to record the quantity and quality of work produced. At the end of the second week, compare the last ten days to the pre-currency data you collected.

THIRD WEEK

Follow the procedures outlined for the second week. Open the store on the last day of each school week and maintain this schedule through the remainder of the year. While evaluating student progress, make a concentrated effort to refine your approach with any student who is not producing a large amount of high-quality work.

REMAINDER OF THE YEAR

Because the students are now familiar with the currency system, much less effort will be necessary to introduce it into other academic areas. Begin to do so gradually.

EXAMPLE 3: SIXTH-GRADE SOCIAL STUDIES

This example details a sixth-grade classroom in which approximately 45 minutes a day are devoted to teaching social studies to 30 students. The educational approach used features large-group instruction, small-group instruction, and individual projects. An aide's help is beneficial, although not essential.

FIRST DAY

Making and using the money. Use $1, $5, $10, and $20 bills.
Planning the activities. Allow the first 15 minutes for explaining the new system and for answering questions. Be sure to tell the students how they can earn and spend the money. Perhaps the best approach is to ask for attention. As they give their attention, reward each of them with a $1 bill. Sixth graders usually catch on quickly and make many valuable and unusual suggestions about the new system's possibilities. In this 15-minute period, the students should be rewarded about five times for their attention and cooperation. Become accustomed to paying, talking, and teaching at the same time. If you wait until you have paid everyone before continuing the topic of conversation, you will lose too much time to make using the money practical.

In the next 15 minutes, present a large-group activity with the potential for at least $20 in rewards. Use a large-group activity answer sheet containing four questions related to the topic being discussed. All the students can answer each question; consequently, all students will be rewarded for participating. Give every student the opportunity to become involved and then give rewards for that involvement. If you do not use a large-group activity answer sheet, you may find that only the brighter and more vocal students are being rewarded.

In the last 15 minutes, open the store so that students can spend their money. If possible, extend the time so that each student has an opportunity to browse and purchase. If you cannot extend the period, hurry the students through. Always give every student an opportunity to visit the store. Students who make their purchases quickly can begin to discuss economic projects similar to those in adult society.

Prepare materials. The materials needed on the first day are the money—$1, $5, $10, and $20 bills; the large-group activity answer sheet; and the store and its contents (see Chapter 7).

Pay students for work completed. Assign half the students to the aide, and pay the other half yourself. When correcting answer sheets, minimize the delay between the completion of work, the correction, and the payoff. The use of stand-up flags (see Figure 9.2) is helpful. You and the aide can thus move from flag to flag, correcting and paying. Reserve hand raising for questions and requests for assistance.

Give students an opportunity to spend the money. Each student should have $25 to spend. Stock the store with sufficient items priced around $25 so as to give each student an opportunity to buy something. Many higher-priced items can also be displayed, since many of your students will understand the concept of saving. We recommend that the aide operate the store

Completed Work			
Name: Johnny Smith			
Date	Assigned Work Completed	Continued Progress	Participation and Attitude Scale 1–5*
10–4	No	No	1
10–5	Yes	Yes	2
10–6	Yes	Yes	3
10–7	Yes	Yes	4
10–8	Yes	Yes	5
*1 = poor; 5 = good			

Figure 9–6. Form for Recording Completed Work.

initially. She should use a record sheet similar to that seen in Figure 9.3 so that popular and not-so-popular items can be identified. By having the aide operate the store, you will be free to discuss projects with the students.

Evaluate student progress. Prior to establishing the currency system, collect between five and ten days of data on each student. (Figure 9.6 illustrates one method of recording this information.) Since social studies work cannot be as specifically measured as math and reading, the data sheet emphasizes your subjective opinions of the child's work. If the currency economy is motivating your students, you will see an increase in work being turned in as well as in academic and creative progress. Records of the quantity and quality of work produced on the first day should be kept for later comparison.

SECOND DAY

Making and using the money. Continue to use $1, $5, $10, and $20 bills. Introduce $50, $100, $500, and $1,000 bills as soon as the students are ready, both conceptually and financially.

Plan the activities. Briefly mention that the new system is still in effect, and then proceed with large-group instruction. Follow the procedure outlined for Day One. In the next 15 minutes, allow the students to work in small groups and explore the potential of their new system. Tell the students you will pay $1 for every idea their group can list on paper about the potential uses of the money. Also indicate you will pay a bonus of $10 to each member of the group who writes the most legible ideas. The time limit for this activity should be ten minutes. In the last 15 minutes, open up the store. Follow the procedure outlined for Day One.

Prepare materials. The materials needed for the second day are the money and large-group activity worksheets.

Pay students for work completed. Follow the procedures outlined for Day One.

Give students an opportunity to spend the money. The store should be stocked with many novel items at a variety of prices. Because of the ability to earn and the potential for saving, the concept of a student-operated bank should be explored (see Chapter 8). Continue to record the quality and quantity of work produced, as it will be needed for analysis later on.

THIRD DAY

Follow the general procedures outlined for Day Two, but vary the small-group activities and begin to emphasize individual projects. Try to structure your session loosely so that each student has the potential to make about $50 per period.

FOURTH DAY

Follow the general procedure outlined for Day Three. Try to get the students interested in forming small businesses for their individual projects.

FIFTH DAY

Follow the general procedure outlined for Day Two, but introduce the idea of a classroom government.

SECOND WEEK

The loose structure of this approach relies heavily on the students' interest and enthusiasm. By this time, the students should be suggesting ways to earn money. Thus, within the afternoon structure, your responsibility is to provide them with guidance, information, and material that will encourage their interest and enthusiasm. Continue to find areas that deserve payment so that the students have a continuous source of income. Stock the store with items such as shoe polish. (Students could then buy the shoe polish and sell shoeshines.) Promote, encourage, and pay off their ingenuity. Life in the classroom should begin to take on real-life meaning.

THIRD WEEK

Follow the basic procedures outlined to implement the currency-based economy in other academic areas.

CHAPTER 10

Back to Basics

I n the excitement and enthusiasm of converting a token system to a currency-based token system, basic reinforcement principles may be forgotten or misapplied. This chapter reviews and reemphasizes the basic tenets of what makes the system work and how to implement it properly. Historically, as previously stated, token systems have been used for two reasons: behavioral control and enhancing motivation.

Behavioral Control

Typically, teachers are concerned about controlling behaviors such as talking out in class at inappropriate times, leaving one's seat at inappropriate times, aggressiveness, and creating distractions. The best way to explain how token systems have been used to make children more manageable is by illustration and example.

Let's begin with talking out without permission. Alfago talks out constantly. If we are to approach him positively, we must first identify a *positive* behavior that is incompatible with talking out. If we only work with the negative talking out, we have no choice but to deal negatively with him. Our goal is to minimize or eliminate his talking-out behavior. We have only two choices: ignore the behavior or punish Alfago every time he exhibits it. Punishment can range from a mild verbal reprimand to a trip to time-out. It is important to note that the attempt to control a negative behavior such as talking out requires negative measures when the behavior is dealt with directly.

The positive option is to find a behavior that is incompatible with Alfago's talking out, and then reduce the talking out by increasing the incompatible one. For instance, the positive behavior we choose may be keeping quiet or appropriate talking behaviors, under the assumption that there will be less time for talking out inappropriately. This is typically how the problem could be handled using a token economy. Since Alfago talks out constantly, the challenge will be to catch him in a moment of silence, or at a time when he is responding appropriately. At the precise second he exhibits the desired behavior, immediate reinforcement should be applied. In a token system, this can be accomplished by dispensing the token and simultaneously praising him. Praise not only increases the power of the tangible reinforcement, but it also gives the teacher an opportunity to tell Alfago what he did that won approval. An alternative approach may be necessary if catching Alfago when he exhibits quiet behavior is not a realistic possibility. Applying this option, the teacher can use the same strategy of reinforcement on a proximate peer, so that Alfago can observe the benefits of appropriate behavior. Using either or both techniques, increases appropriate responses or quiet behavior and decreases talking out.

Notice that the same procedures can be used with out-of-seat behavior. Again, the options of ignoring and punishing are available, but let's see how the token system can be used instead. We have determined that Susan's habit of getting up and wandering around the room not only takes time from her work, but also distracts the rest of the class. The problem and its solution can be approached in two ways. First, Susan can be reinforced immediately when she returns to her seat after a period of wandering. Second, a time duration record of total minutes/seconds in her seat can be reinforced at set intervals. In either case, a combination of praise and token reinforcement should be presented to Susan frequently. As with Alfago, Susan can obtain rewards by exhibiting a desirable behavior incompatible with her undesirable one. We have a clear idea of what the behavior is in both situations; we can work to decrease their occurrence.

Controlling behavior becomes more difficult when its terminology may include a large repertoire of specific behaviors. *Aggressiveness* is an example. It may include hitting, kicking, biting, swearing, and threatening. If we describe Clint as an aggressive child, we have much less information to work with than if we determine he repeatedly pushes his peers whenever the class lines up. When we define the target behavior—pushing in line—we can begin to bring it under control. First, we find a behavior incompatible with pushing. This behavior might be walking to the line while keeping his hands to himself. It is defined and can be observed. We can easily tell whether Clint is performing this positive behavior, and we can reinforce him immediately after he completes the action that is incompatible with pushing.

Distractibility is another term that connotes a wide variety of behaviors and thus needs to be defined in objective terms. If we say Willie is *distractible*, we picture a hyperactive, jumpy kid who cannot get any work done. But we do not know which specific behavior must be modified to improve his ability to complete his academic work. Possibly, Willie stares out the window, cannot concentrate on the task, listens to everything said in the room, or attends to aspects of his worksheet or the classroom that are irrelevant to the task he should be performing. If we can identify one behavior such as staring out the window as our target, then we can identify incompatible behavior and try to increase it. If the amount of time Willie attends to the paper on his desk increases, the amount of time he gazes out the window must decrease. Because a token economy is based on immediate reinforcement of desired behavior, it provides the teacher with a vehicle for the control, and hopefully, Willie's distractibility can be eliminated.

Before completing our discussion on control, we should mention that some teachers elect to use their token system negatively by simply fining the misbehaving student a certain number of tokens each time he misbehaves: e.g., every time Alfago talks out, he could be fined five tokens. Several problems arise with this approach. We suggest that the beginning token economist use the tokens only in a positive manner. If a fine is necessary, a class discussion of how much each fine should be may facilitate its acceptance and hence its effectiveness.

MOTIVATION

Using tokens for motivational purposes is somewhat easier than using them for purposes of control. The basic idea is to motivate the student to do his academic assignments. As an example, we will discuss the completion of seatwork. The two problems are completing the work and the accuracy of the work completed.

Figure 10.1 shows a worksheet that has been completed in a token-economy classroom. Naturally, the worksheet given to the child should reflect his current ability. Each worksheet can be assigned a value based on the time needed to complete the work, the relative difficulty of the work, and the financial status of the economy being operated.

Several optional payoff plans have been used. Payoff for simply completing the worksheet will reinforce rapid work, but it may produce impulsive, inaccurate answers. Payoff for

Completed and paid worksheet

Name __Jim Kent__

Date __Mar 10, 2016__

Contract: Completion __$5   pd 3–10–16__

              100% Right __$5   pd 3–11–16__

$$
\begin{array}{cccc}
6 & 7 & 9 & 8 \\
+\,5 & +\,8 & +\,4 & +\,3 \\
\hline
11 & 15 & \cancel{14} & 11 \\
 & & 13 & \\
\end{array}
$$

$$
\begin{array}{cccc}
2 & 8 & 6 & 5 \\
+\,9 & +\,8 & +\,9 & +\,8 \\
\hline
11 & \cancel{15} & 15 & 13 \\
 & 16 & & \\
\end{array}
$$

Figure 10–1. Completed and Paid Worksheet.

100 percent accuracy alone will reinforce checking and meticulous responses, but may discourage students unable to meet this criterion.

Compromises between the two extremes can help to reinforce both quantity and quality of output. Setting a more realistic criterion—e.g., 90 percent—is one option. However, the most preferable payoff schedule allots a specific number of dollars (tokens) for completion and an additional amount for 100 percent accuracy. With this system, the student is reinforced immediately for finishing his work; in addition, he receives a bonus for correcting his mistakes.

Payoffs can be made at the time the student completes the work or after a daily checking of his work folder. By waiting until she has checked the folder of daily worksheets, the teacher has an opportunity to correct the previous day's assignments and then integrate them into the following day's work. Both arrangements will greatly facilitate individualization of the instruction. With either procedure, she should devise a way of marking the sheets that have been corrected and paid off. By using a rubber stamp or distinctly colored ink to mark the worksheet "paid," she will avoid paying off the same work twice. The worksheet in Figure 10.1 has been marked to show that the student has been paid for completing his work, as well as being given a bonus for 100 percent accuracy.

Three important considerations arise from the discussion on control and motivation through the token economy.

1. <u>Identification of the behavior in question.</u> To deal with a problem situation, it is essential to choose specific target behaviors—those that are observable and can be objectified—rather than general personality characteristics.
2. <u>Use of incompatible behaviors.</u> To avoid dealing with the negative aspects of a situation through punishment, a decrease in the occurrence of the undesirable behavior can be achieved by specifying and reinforcing a positive, incompatible behavior. An increase in the occurrence of a truly incompatible behavior will necessitate a reduction of the undesirable one.
3. <u>Immediacy of payoffs.</u> For the child to understand exactly what he is being reinforced for, the payoff must be given immediately. If he has to wait too long, he may forget why he is being reinforced. A delayed payoff can also result in the inadvertent reinforcement of a different behavior that occurred after the desired one.

In the token economy, immediate payoff can be illustrated by an example of class participation. If a child is paid immediately for responding with an appropriate answer, there will be little doubt in his mind about why he has been paid. However, if the teacher waits until the end of the period to pay the child, she runs the risk of reinforcing him for any number of undesirable behaviors that may have taken place during this time. Accidental reinforcement of the wrong behavior may distort the child's perception of the teacher's standards and thus decrease his motivation to do well.

The currency-based token economy continues the tradition of assisting teachers with classroom management and motivation. As the currency system expands the process from a method of *how* to teach to a curricular concept of *what* to teach, the teacher must not lose sight of the system's basic roots and power.

CHAPTER 11

Personal Growth

By this time, you have a pretty good idea about whether a currency-based token economy is your sort of thing. If you plan to use the currency system for traditional control and motivation purposes, be careful and be precise because it is powerful enough to cause problems as well as solve problems. However, if you plan to use the currency-based system to teach content—that is, use it as a part of the curriculum—then it is no more harmful than selecting a reading or math series. The same common sense and professional judgment must be exercised in implementing a currency economy as for any other curricular component. But whatever the currency system is used for—control, motivation, or curricular purposes—some developmental aspects must be addressed.

Levels of Development

After implementing several currency-based token economies in the elementary grades and in middle schools and high schools, the authors have witnessed several characteristics common to all currency-based systems. These characteristics appear to be developmental: i.e., one precedes the other, and they are important to discuss. Although this chapter may lack scientific sophistication and the data may be far from conclusive, the observations considered seem obvious. For instance, even though the students entering a currency-based economy come from different backgrounds and social strata and have different intellectual and chronological ages, they appear to proceed through similar stages of development, ranging from the amassing and squandering of tokens to a reluctance to accept currency. At one extreme, children try to get as much currency as quickly as they can and exchange it as quickly as possible for cheap, edible items. At the other extreme, there are other children, who, after living in the economy for a year or more, actually say they don't need currency anymore. If persuaded to accept the currency, they either give it away, bank it and never spend it, or use it to buy things for others. This phenomenon is interesting because one would normally think that once children experience the economic system they would perpetuate its existence. The truth is, however, that some children actually outgrow the system and begin to reason as some adults do (e.g., "I don't need to have two cars in my garage; furthermore, I don't need to drive a gas-eating luxury car. A small economy car will suffice; there are many more important things in life than material possessions: for instance, people, friendship, loving, clean air, peace, unpolluted water, trees, etc.").

AMASSING AND SQUANDERING

During the initial stages of implementing a currency-based token economy, we have found that large numbers of students may amass and squander tokens. At the outset, this kind of student works like a beaver; as he earns tokens, he immediately stuffs them into his desk or pocket. He seems compelled to get as many tokens as quickly as he can. He smiles frequently as he accumulates currency. This student also likes to visit the store often to exchange this currency for merchandise. Inevitably, he buys edibles and often devours them before leaving the store. It is interesting that this conspicuous consumer is found at all grade levels, from first and second grade to middle school and high school.

In schoolwork, these amassing/squandering students seem to respond immediately and often are described as impulsive. When currency is issued for completing a task, they sometimes respond quickly; they guess rather than think things out and frequently give the wrong answers. Therefore, it is important to include a variety of ways of earning currency through correct responses, rather than through task completion alone.

These students become very excited when going to the store. They often run to the store, buy their merchandise quickly, and gobble it up. Because these students behave so impulsively (or primitively), many teachers discontinue the currency system because they simply don't want to perpetuate this type of animalistic behavior. On the other hand, our experience has been that within a few weeks, the overwhelming majority of these impulsive students begin to slow down and purchase more expensive items. When an individual begins to consider items that cost more, he must consider the concept of saving. Saving will mean fewer trips to the store or not buying something on every visit. Thus, students begin to experience what it is actually like to delay gratification. Most of them begin to save their money. Furthermore, most of them figure this out on their own and learn to delay gratification as well. However, a few of these students are unable to save their money because it burns a hole in their pocket.

DELAYING GRATIFICATION

Some students approach the teacher dejectedly and clearly state, "I want the ones on the higher shelves (the more expensive items), but when I get in the store I just have to spend." It may be beneficial to teach these students how to save and thus how to delay gratification. Keep in mind that most students move from the immediate-edible-consuming stage to the delaying gratification-saving stage without any coaxing or help from the teacher. Also, many students enter this saving stage at the beginning.

When students need help in learning how to save or delay gratification, there are several alternatives to consider. One obvious way to deal with the problem is to open the store only two days a week or one day a week instead of every day, which forces the student to wait. Some students have trouble saving because they don't understand numerical concepts. For instance, some students have difficulty understanding what $10 (or tokens) versus $50 (or tokens) versus $100 (or tokens) will buy.

One teacher taught a child to understand the concept of 100 as follows. The child found an item he said he wanted. The item was immediately priced at $100 and placed in the store (on reserve) for the child. The teacher made a grid of 100 squares on a piece of 8½"-×-11" paper (ten squares across and ten squares down). At the end of the first day, the child counted his dollars and found he had $38. Thirty-eight squares were crossed out, and he was shown that he still needed $62 to buy the coveted item. At the end of the second day, he added $32 to the $38 and was shown that he still needed $30. On the third day, he purchased the item. As mentioned previously, most students learn this concept on their own with little help, but if a child has some difficulty catching on to the numerical system, a direct approach may be used to facilitate learning.

In some cases, the child understands the numerical concept, but simply is unable to save for the thing he says he wants. In this situation, the items can be rented, or parts of the items can be purchased one at a time. For example, a child in one class wanted to build a model car, but couldn't seem to save enough tokens to purchase the kit. As a compromise, the pieces of the model were sold separately. At the end of the first day, for instance, he might purchase the wheels, the engine, or the glue. In a somewhat more elaborate system, a bicycle was purchased in this manner and was actually built in the corner of the classroom.

If the cherished item cannot be disassembled, you may wish to consider taking a picture of the item, cutting the picture up into pieces, and selling the pieces to the student. When the student has purchased all the pieces, he may exchange them for the item.

Although saving can be considered a value-related concept and thus is not encouraged by some teachers, there is something to be said for teaching the concept. After the concept has been learned, you can leave it up to the individual child to decide whether or not he will save.

Many students, after learning how to save and delay gratification, begin to discuss and think out their purchases. In other words, they become thinking consumers rather than merely responding consumers. When students begin talking about their future purchases with fellow students, the concept of sharing begins to evolve.

SHARING

The student who can share is less possessive and gradually learns the pleasure and hardships of sharing. At first, it usually takes the form of the sharing of ideas, which is seldom harmful and in most systems evolves naturally. One of the few times it becomes harmful is when a student shares with a friend the fact that he desires an item and the friend purchases the item first. This problem is eliminated when several identical items are stocked or when a layaway plan is initiated.

The sharing of ideas is later followed by the sharing of items; in other words, the students allow their friends to play with their purchased possessions. Also, it is not uncommon for students to pool their money and buy an item collectively. This most certainly is a higher-level process, and a considerable amount of learning takes place in these cooperative ventures. The next stage of development seems to be the actual purchasing of an item for another person.

GIVING

Buying gifts for others usually begins within the family. A student in the currency-based economy may buy a present for a brother or sister or his mother or father, usually for a birthday or anniversary. However, this behavior may be followed by the purchase of gifts for no apparent reason. This giving behavior later spreads to nonrelatives within and outside the classroom.

At the middle school and high school levels, it is difficult to know exactly what to have in the store, since older students usually have learned to appreciate expensive items. However, with little difficulty, a soda shop can be set up in the corner of the room, and you might be surprised at how much middle school and high school students enjoy taking a friend for a Coke or sundae. Also, they often enjoy designing the space itself.

Another form of giving is tutoring. Students can pay a classmate for tutorial help, and of course it is possible for the teacher to pay students to perform tutorial tasks.

One sad thing is to see a student who tries to buy friends. Although this behavior is difficult for the average teacher to witness without intervening, these students eventually wise up and either seek different friends or use different skills for acquiring friends.

REFUSING PAYMENT

In the last stage, a student progresses over a period of time (usually a year or more) to the point where he decides he doesn't want any money and says quite frankly, "I don't need money anymore." This student begins to see through the system and begins to value other things in his school life. He surrounds himself with a few close friends, yet doesn't go out of his way to be liked. He seems to be confident and independent. Sometimes, this student becomes arrogant and opposes or rebels against the commercialization of traditions such as Christmas, Easter, and Valentine's Day. This individual usually doesn't make an issue out of not accepting currency; in fact, he will often simply bank it and never spend it.

This level of development should not be confused with the student who tries to upset or test the system. He likes to earn money, but has become frustrated because he can't earn enough or is upset because others are earning more than he is. This rebellious student is still functioning at the gratification-delay stage and will gradually succumb to the system. He should not be confused with the more mature payment-refusing student.

The maturing student who refuses currency experiences a kind of insight or an "aha" moment. He begins to look at life differently and formulate new goals. This individual seems to be on his way to independent thought, self-evaluation, and possibly self-actualization. In other words, he appears to be more internally motivated rather than externally motivated.

The question that comes to mind is: Can this independent, mature, self-actualized thinking and behavior be taught in the abstract, or does it have to be experienced directly? At present, we are witnessing attempts to teach various values through commercial types of curricular materials. These commercial materials feature lessons such as the following: "How do I make decisions? Am I an intelligent consumer? Do I want to use drugs? How do I feel about drinking? Should I smoke? Do I need laws? Am I prejudiced? What should I do about pollution? What is my role as a citizen? What career will I choose? What are my goals in life?"

All these commercial materials approach the teaching of values and the teaching of decision making as though they were subject matter. We do not mean to imply that these issues are not legitimate subject matter; in fact, many of them can probably be taught directly. However, if a school can provide an environment that allows students an opportunity to *experience* problem-solving related to values—in addition to being taught values directly as subject matter—then maybe it should try to do so.

To date, concepts such as delayed gratification, sharing, giving, and possibly the value of independence are rarely taught in the elementary school. They may be discussed from time to time, but usually only when a crisis arises. At the middle school and high school levels, these concepts once again may only be discussed in crisis situations or possibly may be taught somewhat directly as subject matter in a psychology, philosophy, or values course.

Our suggestion is that possibly these concepts may best be *experienced* directly through a currency-based economy and may be viewed as developmental, rather than learned or experienced in isolation. Because these stages of development within a token economy just seem to evolve, they need not be forced on any student. Also, these stages are so important that it may be wrong to assume all individuals will experience them outside the classroom. It is our belief that many adults continue to function predominantly at the stage of delayed gratification or sharing. If this is so, the reason may be that they have not had the opportunity to explore and experience these stages extensively enough to be able to move to the next stage. This possible explanation is worth considering and pondering.

Sharing Two Experiences

We would like to stop here for a moment and share two experiences that had a substantial impact on us. The first deals with stealing.

STEALING

Stealing seems to be inevitable when a currency system is established. During our initial experience with the system, our concern was to minimize theft, if not eliminate it. This was easily done by initialing the currency given to the suspected thief: e.g., his initials were placed on the currency he earned. Furthermore, he could only cash in money containing his initials. The stealing quickly diminishes when the student finds nothing is to be gained by stealing.

Next, we decided that because stealing takes place in the real world, each student should be responsible for keeping track of his own money. Most children quickly took steps to protect their possessions. However, among some children, this promoted distrust in fellow classmates. We decided to study stealing and its impact on children in more depth. We interviewed over 100 first- and second-grade children and informally questioned each one about his thoughts on stealing. Two important developments came out of the interviewing process: The first dealt with the children's reaction to Robin Hood; the second related to when stealing would be all right.

Surprisingly, when questioned about Robin Hood (a subject that had not been mentioned in class), almost every student not only knew of him, but responded: "He stole from the rich and he gave to the poor." When asked about whether this was all right, a few said yes, a few said no, and a few didn't know. However, several students indicated that his actions were no longer necessary because the government now gives money to the poor. This statement impressed us, since most of the students who made this response were on a free or reduced-cost lunch program.

When we asked if there was ever a time when stealing would be okay, we meant to imply a situation when it would be permissible. More than half the students reported: "Yes, at recess when the teacher is out of the room," or "Yes, at night when people are asleep." This also impressed us because these first- and second-graders already had learned informally and indirectly that what was wrong with stealing was getting caught.

After encountering these responses to Robin Hood and the accountability of stealing, we began to discuss stealing in the classroom. This was relevant, since stealing was occurring in the currency economy. We were amazed by the level at which first- and second-grade children were able to discuss the issue. As a result, our concern about stealing in a currency-based economy has shifted from minimizing or extinguishing stealing to an in-depth discussion of stealing. We are not necessarily trying to conclude that stealing is either right or wrong or good or bad, but a discussion of the various situations in which stealing may occur seems to be important to young children themselves.

CONFUSED CONSUMER

A second situation that had an impact on us was the time a second-grader decided she wanted to save for a doll that was displayed in the store. She verbally expressed a strong desire for it, so we put it on layaway for her. The doll was made of plastic and was actually very inexpensive (but high cost in currency based dollars), yet this student seemed to crave it. Each week, she went to the store to admire the doll and then returned to her room and resumed her work. This went on for about eight or nine weeks, until she finally had saved enough money to buy the doll. She went to the store, counted out the money, one bill at a time, and handed the money to the clerk in exchange for the doll. She picked up the doll and ran her hands all over it, as if to memorize every square inch. Her eyes began to water and she walked slowly back to class. She sat down at her desk and continued to rub her hands over the doll. Finally, after several minutes, she carefully placed the doll into her desk and took out her math paper. She would do a couple of math problems and then reach in her desk, pull out the doll, and look at it. After looking at the doll for a short time, she would return it and continue working, and then repeat the process all over again. After this had gone on for a while, she raised her hand. When the teacher went over to her and asked what she wanted, the student asked this question: "How come I wanted the doll so bad when it was in the store, but now that I have it, it's nothing?"

How does one answer a question such as that? This teacher, rightly or wrongly, responded: "I don't know, but it has happened to me, too." She then hugged the student and returned to her teaching. Our thought at the time was that this child had experienced an insight which many individuals don't experience until they are adults, earning their own salaries in the very real world.

Instances such as these have made us realize how close we are to injecting relevance into education, yet how far we are from understanding how to facilitate the development of independent thinkers. Now we want to turn our attention to the education of intellectually well-endowed students.

Using Currency With Gifted Children

Token systems have been used predominantly with students who experience difficulty in learning through traditional methods in traditional classroom settings. The currency system lends itself to teaching everyone, including intellectually, emotionally, and academically superior students. In fact, the teaching of social leadership skills could be approached through the establishment of a currency-based token system. Social leadership skills are learned through a trial-and-error process in clubs, athletics, and informal groups.

Simulated management games have been used by some businesses to facilitate the development of leadership skills. These approaches use mock situations in which students play the role of manager. These future leaders make policies, implement decisions, and analyze the consequences of their actions. We believe that a currency-based token economy is one outgrowth of simulated management games.

Although there is seldom unanimous agreement about which skills are necessary for personal adjustment, everyone seems to agree that many problems exist in our society that need to be solved. War, crime, drugs, alcoholism, overpopulation, overcrowding, pollution, snarled transportation, and political corruption threaten our survival. Teachers can and must use their abilities to teach not only the academic subjects needed to survive in society, but also how to use this information to change society for the better. Problem solving of any kind is best learned when the learner is involved in finding solutions through personal experience. One way in which societal problems can be resolved by future generations is to provide students with opportunities to grapple with issues, conflicts, triumphs, disappointments, and power in the social microcosm the classroom represents.

Although we do not mean to imply that gifted children should be forced into attempting to solve society's problems or that their intellectual talents should be harnessed for society's own selfish gains, voluminous evidence indicates that the gifted are especially receptive to the influence of peers and authority. Parents, teachers, and peers do have an impact on the decisions of most gifted individuals. During the Sputnik era in the late 1950s, gifted persons were enticed into pursuing degrees and vocations in the physical sciences. The pressing need today is to objectify information in the social sciences, and if the gifted are properly instructed in our educational settings, they may find it gratifying as well as challenging to solve society's problems. The concept of a currency-based token economy might lend itself to addressing these perplexing issues.

CONCLUSION

The currency-based token economy is a system that can be beneficial to handicapped, normal, and gifted students. This system can be implemented for all age groups, from first through twelfth grades. It can motivate unmotivated children and control uncontrollable children. It can provide a curricular device for teaching aspects of career education—not to mention addition, subtraction, multiplication, and division. It even lends itself to the teaching of complex concepts such as honesty and other values. Even more important, it has the potential to help individuals along the developmental path from egocentricity to a sharing, giving, self-awareness that may cultivate independence and even approach some degree of self-actualization.

We live in a time when large segments of the population are questioning the materialistic values of the top one percent. People are asking what life is all about, why we are here, what is our purpose in life, and the like. Issues are raised concerning inflation, recession, and depression. However, these issues take on different meanings to those who have experienced satisfaction in the consumption of material possessions. There is a vast difference between the family that decides to return to the land to live a simple, uncomplicated life—knowing they have the skills to compete in an industrialized, computerized world—versus the family that finds itself trapped in poverty—ignorant and deprived of the skills needed to compete in our complex world. Although both families live meager lives, one is rich and substantive, while the other is almost pitiful. The difference hinges on choice: one family has a choice and knows one exists; the other is a pawn and can only respond to outside pressures.

The currency-based economy has the potential to teach every child the skills necessary for competing and surviving in today's society. It appears to us that the individuals who are the happiest, most well adjusted, and who live fully functioning lives are those who have learned the following: "I don't need a chicken in every pot, I don't need two cars in my garage, and I don't need a house in the suburbs." These individuals know themselves. They are less likely to be manipulated by others. They can be happy and lead substantive lives with no car, or, yes, even with a limousine! They may have a chicken in their pot whenever they want, two cars, and a house bigger than they need, but they know that the material things are not what make them happy. They can lead meaningful lives on a farm, in a ghetto, and even in a suburb. Why? Because they are in control of themselves and are not subject to the whims of external events. In other words, they have learned to know their own strengths and weaknesses. They are inquisitive, curious, and fun loving. These people no longer hunger for money, power, or esteem; they can spend money wisely, use their position appropriately, and their concept of self is neither inflated nor deflated. These individuals may have ambition, yet they are not ambitious.

How can a currency-based token economy facilitate this type of evolution? We believe the answer is: by assisting students through the stages of development—from amassing and squandering; to delaying gratification, sharing, and giving; to the actual devaluation of the importance of currency. This last step may, in fact, be the ultimate goal of the currency economy, or for that matter, the goal of education—*satiation of external reinforcers*. In other words, the goal may be to help students attain a level of psychological existence in which they no longer need (or are compelled) to have material possessions. Although they may know how to acquire these possessions and may know how to use them, they are not enslaved by these possessions. In summary, the final goal may be to satiate young children or adolescents on external reinforcers. (See Figure 11.1 below.) This strategy is worth further discussion and possibly worth additional research.

Developmental hierarchy of a currency-based token economy

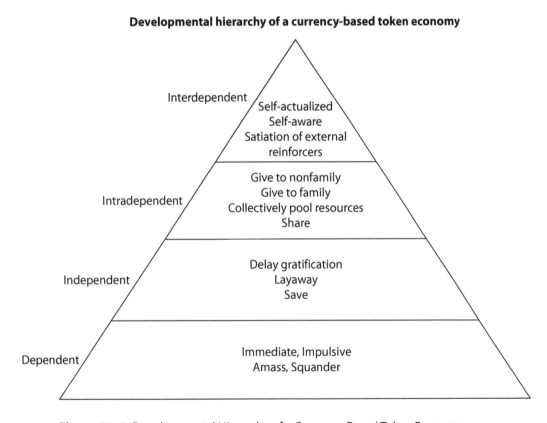

Figure 11–1. Developmental Hierarchy of a Currency-Based Token Economy.

CHAPTER 12

Literature

R esearch on the use of token economies is well established. The following is a comprehensive review of over 100 professional publications, ranging from the 1960s to the present day. Each publication and the published abstract or a direct web link to the abstract are listed below.

Alter, P. (2012). Helping students with emotional and behavioral disorders solve mathematics word problems. *Preventing School Failure*, 56, 55–64. doi:10.1080/1045988X.2011.565283

The author presents a strategy for helping students with emotional and behavioral disorders become more proficient at solving math word problems. Math word problems require students to go beyond simple computation in mathematics (e.g., adding, subtracting, multiplying, and dividing) and use higher-level reasoning that includes recognizing relevant information, disregarding irrelevant information, and choosing the correct arithmetic operation. By teaching a multistep problem-solving strategy and reinforcing completion of each step through a token economy, four students improved in their math problem-solving ability and their overall on-task behavior during the work sessions. In addition, one student transitioned from a teacher-driven token economy to use the token economy as a self-monitoring system. The author describes this strategy and the accompanying token economy system and provides the results of the intervention for four students.

Axelrod, S. (1971). Token reinforcement programs in special classes. *Exceptional Children, 37*, 371–378.

Reviews token reinforcement programs in the special education classroom and indicates that positive results were almost invariably obtained, even with different types of target behaviors and various kinds of populations, including handicapped teenagers, urban underachievers, dropouts, the learning and reading disabled, and the emotionally disturbed. It is suggested that ways be devised of withdrawing tokens without interruption of progress and that greater use be made of reinforcers already existing in the classroom. (PsycINFO Database Record (c) 2012 APA, all rights reserved)

Ayllon, T., & Azrin, N. H. (1968). *The token economy: A motivational system for therapy and rehabilitation*. New York: Appleton-Century-Crofts.

No abstract is available for this journal article.

Baine, D. A. (1973). Beyond the token economy. *Mental Retardation Bulletin, 1*(3), 60–64.

Examines the concepts underlying token economy systems employed for behavior modification and change. It is noted that the durability of behavior changes following removal of the use of tokens is suspect, and that studies of long-term behavior change after discontinuation of the token economy are essentially nonexistent. Suggestions (specific individual praise; self-evaluation) are offered for improving the maintenance and generalization of behavior changes. (PsycINFO Database Record (c) 2012 APA, all rights reserved)

Balcerzak, W. S., & Siddall, J. W. (1974). A brief discussion of a model for improving the cost effectiveness of a token economy in a rehabilitation setting. *Journal of Applied Behavior Analysis, 7,* 501–504.

No abstract is available for this journal article. http://onlinelibrary.wiley.com/doi/10.1901/jaba.1974.7-501/abstract

Barkley, R., Hastings, J., Tousel, R., & Tousel, S. (1976). Evaluation of a token system for juvenile delinquents in a residential setting. *Journal of Behavior Therapy and Experimental Psychiatry, 7,* 227–230.

The influence of a token economy in a residential treatment facility for delinquents was evaluated in three areas of behavior: (a) in-house chore performance; (b) littering in the facility; and (c) school performance as reflected in daily evaluations by teachers. Chore performance and littering were influenced favorably by the token system. School performance, however, appeared to be unaffected by the reversal of the token program. Reasons for this finding are discussed and the need underscored that existing token systems evaluate the effectiveness of their program contingencies on a regular basis.

Bassett, J. E., & Blanchard, E. B. (1977). The effect of the absence of close supervision on the use of response cost in a prison token economy. *Journal of Applied Behavior Analysis, 10,* 375–379.

A naturally occurring experiment, in which direct supervision of a token economy in a penal system was removed and reinstated, is reported. A retrospective analysis reveals that in the absence of close supervision, the use of response cost rose dramatically, both in terms of categories of behaviors for which response costs were levied and in the frequency of their use. The return of direct supervision led to a decreased use and an end to the growth of categories of behaviors punished.

Bippes, R., McLaughlin, T. F., & Williams, R. L. (1986). A classroom token system in a detention center: Effects for academic and social behavior. *Techniques*, vol. 2, issue 2, 126–132.

Examines the effects of a token (point) economy on the reading scores and social behavior ratings of five male delinquent youths (aged 14–16 yrs) in a detention center. Results for reading indicate increased accuracy in reading comprehension and achievement for each subject. Subjective ratings by the staff also suggest improved social behavior in the detention center for three subjects. (28 ref) (PsycINFO Database Record (c) 2012 APA, all rights reserved)

Birnbrauer, J. S., Wolf, M. M., Kidder, J., & Tague, C. E. (1965). Classroom behavior of retarded pupils with token reinforcement. *Journal of Experimental Child Psychology, 2,* 219–235.

It was the practice in an experimental programmed instruction classroom to reinforce correct responses with knowledge of results, verbal approval, and tokens. The tokens, check marks, were exchanged at the end of each class for an item from an array of edibles, inexpensive toys, and school supplies. To determine if the token reinforcement was essential to the relatively high levels of accuracy and rates of studying maintained by the retarded pupils, tokens were not dispensed for a period of at least 21 days and were then reinstated. Daily records of items completed, percentage of errors, and disruptive behavior were kept. During the no-token period, three general patterns of results were obtained: (1) Five of the 15 pupils showed no measurable change in performance. (2) Six pupils increased either markedly in overall percentage of errors or sufficiently to reduce progress in the programs. (3) Four pupils showed an increase in percentage of errors, a decline (or considerable variability) in amount of studying, and an increase in disruptive behavior. Baseline performance was recovered in these ten pupils when token reinforcement was reinstated.

Boniecki, K. A., & Moore, S. (2003). Breaking the silence: Using a token economy to reinforce classroom participation. *Teaching of Psychology, 30*(3), 224–227. doi:10.1207/S15328023TOP3003_05

We propose a procedure for increasing student participation, particularly in large classes. The procedure establishes a token economy in which students earn tokens for participation and then exchange those tokens for extra credit. We evaluated the effectiveness of the procedure by recording the degree of participation in an introductory psychology class before, during, and after implementation of the token economy. Results revealed that the amount of directed and nondirected participation increased during the token economy and returned to baseline after removal of the token economy. Furthermore, students responded faster to questions from the instructor during the token economy than during baseline, and this decrease in response latency continued even after removal of the token economy.

Bourgeois, T. L. (1968). Reinforcement theory in teaching the mentally retarded: A token economy program. *Perspectives in Psychiatric Care, 6*, 17–21.

No abstract is available for this journal article.

Broden, M., Hall, R. V., Dunlap, A., & Clark, R. (1970). Effects of teacher attention and a token reinforcement system in a junior high school special education class. *Exceptional Children, 36*, 341–349.

Employs teacher attention and a token reinforcement system to control a disruptive junior high school special education classroom. Individual and group study levels were recorded during a baseline period. Subsequent experimental periods using teacher attention and/or a token point system increased study levels and decreased disruptive behaviors of class members. Reinforcement of appropriate behaviors was withdrawn during short reversals, producing lowered study rates. Reinstatement of contingencies again resulted in increased study levels. (PsycINFO Database Record (c) 2012 APA, all rights reserved)

Broughton, S. F., & Lahey, B. B. (1978). Direct and collateral effects of positive reinforcement, response cost, and mixed contingencies for academic performance. *Journal of School Psychology, 16*, 126–136. doi:10.1016/0022-4405(78)90051-1

The relative effects of positive reinforcement, response cost, and the two contingencies combined when used as contingencies for correct academic responses were compared on the dependent measures of accuracy of academic performance and level of on-task behavior. Thirty-three fourth- and fifth-grade pupils served as subjects. A combination of between-group and within-group comparisons indicated that all three contingency systems increased academic performance and on-task behavior (even though on-task behavior was never directly reinforced), but differences in effectiveness between the systems were insignificant. Most importantly, treatment effects on academic performance and on-task behavior persisted following abrupt withdrawal of treatments for all three contingency systems. These results confirm earlier speculations that the reinforcement of academic behavior is (a) more likely to positively influence both academic and on-task behavior than in reinforcement of on-task behavior; and (b) is much more resistant to extinction following abrupt termination of the program.

Copyright © 1978 Published by Elsevier Ltd.

Burchard, J. D., & Barrera, F. (1972). An analysis of time-out and response cost in a programmed environment. *Journal of Applied Behavior Analysis, 5*, 271–282.

A group of mildly retarded adolescents with high rates of antisocial behavior was exposed to two parameters of time-out and response cost within the context of a programmed environment. For five of the six subjects, the two higher values (30 tokens response cost, or 30 minutes' time-out) were significantly more suppressive than the lower values (five tokens, or five minutes). For the one remaining subject, there was a strong relationship in the opposite direction. Also, the time-out and response cost of higher value became increasingly more suppressive over time, whereas those of lower value did not. There were few appreciable differences between the time-out and response cost of similar magnitude. A discussion of these results is presented in support of the notion that the functional aversiveness of time-outs (and response costs) appears to be critically dependent upon interactions with the environmental

130

conditions in which they are implemented and the reinforcement histories of the subjects. http://www.ncbi.nlm.nih.gov/pmc/articles/PMC1310763/

Campbell, A., & Anderson, C. M. (2011). Check-in/Check-out: A systematic evaluation and component analysis. *Journal of Applied Behavior Analysis, 44*(2), 315–326.

Tier 2 interventions are implemented similarly across students and thus serve as an efficient and cost-effective method of behavior support in school settings. Check-in/check-out is a Tier 2 intervention with documented effectiveness (e.g., Hawken & Horner, 2003; Todd, Campbell, Meyer, & Horner, 2008). Key features of the intervention include brief morning and afternoon meetings with the intervention coordinator, use of a point card on which the teacher monitors student behavior, and teacher feedback at predetermined times. The present study sought to add to the literature by examining the relative contributions of the teacher-feedback components of check-in/check-out via the use of a component analysis. Working with four children in a general education setting, we first evaluated the effectiveness of the procedure using reversal designs. Next, we systematically removed teacher-feedback components to assess effects on problem behavior and academic engagement. For three of four participants, we were able to remove all teacher-feedback sessions and the point card; for the fourth participant, we removed only two of three teacher-feedback sessions due to time constraints.

Carey, R. G., Mosk, M. D., & Kranchuck, K. B. (1981). Employing overcorrection as a cost contingency in a token economy. *Behavior Research of Severe Developmental Disabilities, 2,* 1016–1025.

An overcorrection procedure and a response cost procedure are employed as cost contingencies in a token economy program, and the performance of six retarded 28- to 40-year-olds (IQs of 50–83 as assessed by the WAIS) is assessed in a multiple-component reversal design for an academic task. The percentage of correct responding and the time spent on-task were recorded as dependent measures. Two subjects received both restitutional and positive practice overcorrection as a consequence for incorrect responding plus token reinforcement for correct responding, and two subjects received a token fine as a consequence for incorrect responding, plus token reinforcement for correct responding. Two control subjects received either no-cost contingency plus contingent token reinforcement or no-cost contingency plus noncontingent token reinforcement. Results show that both overcorrection plus reinforcement and response cost plus reinforcement contingencies were effective in increasing both dependent measures. Neither of the control subjects demonstrated consistent gains in performance.

Cavalier, A. R., Ferretti, R. P., & Hodges, A. E. (1997). Self-management within a classroom token economy for students with learning disabilities. *Research in Developmental Disabilities, 18,* 167–178. doi:10.1016/S0891-4222(96)00045-5

Students with disabilities who are served in restrictive educational settings often display inappropriate behavior that serves to preclude their integration into the mainstream. One approach to managing difficult behavior is a levels system (Smith & Farrell, 1993), which typically consists of a hierarchy of levels in which students must meet increasingly demanding standards of behavior before advancing through the hierarchy. In the present study, two middle school students with learning disabilities participated in a classroom-wide token economy based on a levels system. The levels system, which was used in a self-contained classroom, targeted the acquisition and maintenance of academic skills and social behaviors with the goal of integrating these students into an inclusive classroom. The two participants showed little or no progress within the levels system because of a very high rate of inappropriate verbalizations. Therefore, a self-management system that involved training on the accuracy of self-recording these verbalizations was added to the levels system for these students. In addition, the investigator discussed with these students the consequences of inappropriate behavior and socially appropriate behavioral alternatives. A multiple-baseline-across-subjects experimental design revealed that the intervention resulted in a substantive reduction in inappropriate verbalizations, as well as greater progress through the levels system. Implications of these findings for the use of self-recording within a token economy, the importance of students' accuracy of self-recording, and methodological issues are discussed.

Center, D. B., & Wascom, A. (1984). Transfer of reinforcers: A procedure for enhancing response cost. *Educational and Psychological Research, 4*(1), 19–27.

Conducted a study to determine if the punitive effect of response cost could be increased by transferring token reinforcers from a student engaged in inappropriate behavior to another student engaged in appropriate behavior. Subjects were five white boys, 12–14 yrs old, in a special education class for behavior-disordered children. An ABAB reversal design was used. Analyses indicate that the transfer procedure, relative to the standard procedure of returning the token to a supply container, enhanced the effect of response cost within the token economy. (10 ref) (PsycINFO Database Record (c) 2012 APA, all rights reserved) http://psycnet.apa. org/psycinfo/1985-10798-001

Chen, C. W., & Ma, H. H. (2007). Effects of treatment on disruptive behaviors: A quantitative synthesis of single-subject researches using the PEM approach. *Behavior Analyst Today, 8*(4), 380.

The present study uses the PEM approach to synthesize the effectiveness of treatment on disruptive behaviors and simultaneously tests whether the higher validity of the PEM approach than that of the PND approach is repeatable. A hand search of the *Journal of Applied Behavior Analysis* was conducted, and reference lists from reviewed articles were traced to locate relevant studies. Altogether, 106 single-subject studies, which produced 694 effect sizes, were analyzed. The grand mean of 106 averaged effect sizes was significant. Results demonstrated that the PEM approach was more congruent with the original authors' judgments than the PND approach. Important findings regarding the effectiveness of interventions on the disruptive behaviors are that the strategies of differential reinforcement and the token economy system, along with multi-components intervention, were highly effective. (PsycINFO Database Record (c) 2014 APA, all rights reserved.

Christophersen, E. R., Arnold, C. M., Hill, D. W., & Quilitch, H. R. (1972). The home point system: Token reinforcement procedures for application by parents of children with behavior problems. *Journal of Applied Behavior Analysis, 5,* 485–497.

Parent-child problems within the home are frequently reported to be instances in which children refuse to help with household chores, bicker among themselves, or engage in verbally inappropriate behavior toward their parents. The present study investigates the effects of a token reinforcement program administered by the parents in ameliorating these problems. Two sets of parents, with a total of five children between the ages of five and ten years old, were taught to administer a token economy within their homes. The parents received instruction in specifying desired social and chore behaviors, communicated these behavioral goals to their children, recorded data on their occurrence, and managed a point system backed with reinforcers normally found in the home. The token reinforcement program was shown to have successfully modified 15 problem behaviors in Family 1 and six in Family 2. In addition, the parents rated all 21 behavior changes as significant improvements. These studies indicated that some cooperative parents need only a small amount of professional help to learn to manage their children's behavior problems with token reinforcement procedures.

http://www.ncbi.nlm.nih.gov/pmc/articles/PMC1310790/

Clark, M., Lachowicz, J., & Wolf, M. (1968). A pilot basic education program for school dropouts incorporating a token reinforcement system. *Behavior Research and Therapy, 6,* 183–188.

Five female school dropouts were "hired" to complete remedial workbook assignments. They were paid (via a token system) for the items that they worked correctly. Significant gains were observed in achievement test scores during the two-month program. Experimental analyses with individual students show the token reinforcement system to function as such.

Comaty, J. E., Stasio, M., & Advokat, C. (2001). Analysis of outcome variables of a token economy (TE) treatment program in a state psychiatric hospital: A program evaluation. *Research in Developmental Disabilities, 22,* 233–253.

This study describes the outcome of a token economy treatment applied to two distinct patient populations on the same unit of a state psychiatric hospital: individuals with a dual diagnosis of mental retardation and a DSM-IV Axis I diagnosis of either (a) a severe behavior disorder (BD); or (b) a serious and persistent psychiatric disorder (PD). Results showed that patients in the PD group were more likely to complete the treatment (17/20) than those in the BD group (17/31), who were more likely to be terminated from the program (14/31). Individuals who did not complete the program were distinguished early, within the first three weeks of treatment. These noncompleters received significantly more fines and earned significantly fewer tokens than those who completed the program. At an average of 2.7 years post-discharge, there was no difference in the proportion of PD (12/16), BD completers (9/11), and BD noncompleters (3/7) remaining in the community. These data show that diverse populations of patients can be treated within the same token economy program, thereby improving cost effectiveness. Future research should be directed toward characterizing those patients (e.g., BD) less likely to succeed when they enter treatment and determining if modifications in the program can improve that outcome.

Conyers, C., Miltenberger, R. G., Gubin, A., Barenz, R., Jurgens, M., Sailer, A., Haugen, M., & Kopp, B. (2004). A comparison of response cost and differential reinforcement of other behavior to reduce disruptive behavior in a preschool classroom. *Journal of Applied Behavior Analysis, 37*(3), 411–415.

This study investigates the effectiveness of response cost and differential reinforcement of other behavior (DRO) in reducing the disruptive behaviors of 25 children in a preschool classroom. Using an alternating treatments design, disruptive behavior was reduced when the participants earned tokens for the absence of disruptive behavior (DRO) or lost tokens for the occurrence of disruptive behavior (response cost). Initially, DRO was more successful in reducing the number of disruptive behaviors; however, over time, response cost proved to be more effective.
http://www.ncbi.nlm.nih.gov/pmc/articles/PMC1284517/

Corrigan, P. W. (1995). Use of token economy with seriously mentally ill patients: Criticisms and misconceptions. *Psychiatric Services, 46*, 1258–1263.

Presents common criticisms of the use of token economies in the milieu management of treatment programs for adults and children with severe mental illness. Detractors argue that token economies are ineffective, that their benefits do not readily generalize to other settings, that token economies do not foster individualized treatment plans, that participating in a token economy is humiliating, that token economies are abusive, that concerns about milieu management are unimportant and irrelevant to treatment delivery in the 1990s, and that effective token economies are impractical. Empirical evidence is presented to rebut these misconceptions and criticisms. Three steps in establishing a token economy include identifying target behavior, establishing contingencies for each target, and defining the exchange rules for using the token store. (PsycINFO Database Record (c) 2012 APA, all rights reserved)

Cotler, S. B., Applegate, G., King, L. W., & Kristal, S. (1972). Establishing a token economy program in a state hospital classroom: A lesson in training student and teacher. *Behavior Therapy, 209*, 214–217.

The goals of this study were to establish a program in a state hospital classroom in order to: (A) increase appropriate study behavior; (B) increase the quantity and quality of work output; and (C) train the regular classroom teacher so that he could eventually administer the program on his own. A four-day-per-week token economy program was set up for the teacher's most disruptive class. The program lasted 15 weeks and consisted of three treatment and two baseline phases. During each subsequent treatment phase, the delay between earning points and cashing the points in for backup reinforcers was increased. Students were observed and reinforced twice during each study period (and additionally reinforced after the study period during certain treatment phases). Reinforcers used to initiate and sustain desired behaviors consisted of social approval, points, toys, and candies. Extinction and time-out procedures were used in conjunction with positive reinforcement to reduce disruptive behaviors. Results indicate that appropriate study behavior and quantity of work output increased significantly in the reinforced treatment phases as compared to the baseline phases. However, the last treatment phase of the study is significantly lower in terms of quality of work output as compared to the other four phases. Problems encountered during the study, what factors may have accounted for the decrease in the quality of work output, and how a program of this type might be made even more effective are discussed.

Coundiff, W. E., & Coffman, M. T. (1969). Token changes. *School and Community, 56*, 41.

No abstract is available for this article.

Dalton, A. J., Rubino, C. A., & Hislop, M. W. (1971). Some effects of token rewards on school achievement of children with Down syndrome. *Journal of Applied Behavior Analysis, 6,* 251–259.

> The effectiveness of a token economy system in producing improvement in the academic performance of children with Down syndrome is tested. One group of seven children received token reinforcement for correct responses and showed significant improvement both in arithmetic and language. A second matched group of six children received only verbal praise for correct responses to the same instructional materials and failed to improve in arithmetic, but showed significant gains in language. Retest scores one year later revealed that the Token Group maintained its gains in both subjects, whereas the language performance of the No-Token Group showed a significant decline.

> http://www.ncbi.nlm.nih.gov/pmc/articles/PMC1310832/

Dickerson, F. B., Tenhual, W. N., & Green-Paden, L. D. (2005). The token economy for schizophrenia: Review of the literature and recommendations for future research. *Schizophrenia Research, 75,* 405–416. doi:10.1016/j.schres.2004.08.026

> The token economy is a treatment intervention based on principles of operant conditioning and social learning. Developed in the 1950s and 1960s for long-stay hospital patients, the token economy has fallen out of favor since that time. The current review was undertaken as part of the 2003 update of the schizophrenia treatment recommendations of the Patient Outcomes Research Team (PORT). A total of 13 controlled studies of the token economy was reviewed. As a group, the studies provide evidence of the token economy's effectiveness in increasing the adaptive behaviors of patients with schizophrenia. Most of the studies are limited, however, by methodological shortcomings and by the historical context in which they were performed. More research is needed to determine the specific benefits of the token economy when administered in combination with contemporary psychosocial and psychopharmacological treatments.
> http://www.researchgate.net/publication/7854704_The_token_economy_for_schizophrenia_review_of_the_literature_and_recommendations_for_future_research

Doty, D. W., McInnis, T., & Paul, G. L. (1974). Remediation of negative side effects of an ongoing response cost system with chronic mental patients. *Journal of Applied Behavior Analysis, 7,* 191–198.

http://www.ncbi.nlm.nih.gov/pmc/articles/PMC1311957/

Everett, P. B., Hayward, S. C., & Meyers, A. W. (1974). The effects of a token reinforcement procedure on bus ridership. *Journal of Applied Behavior Analysis, 7,* 1-9.

Tokens, exchangeable for a variety of backup reinforcers, are delivered for several days to all persons boarding a clearly marked campus bus. This procedure increased ridership to 150 percent of baseline. The experiment was carried out to demonstrate the applicability of operant techniques to urban transportation problems. In this study, a token reinforcement procedure was introduced in an attempt to increase bus ridership while holding the costs of reinforcers to a minimum and circumventing the problems of individual satiety and preferences and of delivering cumbersome reinforcers. A methodology for establishing a token-exchange procedure in an "open-field" behavior setting, where the subject population size, geographic location, preferences, age, sex, preferred hours of mobility, etc., are unspecified, is also presented.

Filcheck, H. A., & McNeil, C. B. (2004). The use of token economies in preschool classrooms: Practical and philosophical concerns. *Journal of Early and Intensive Behavior Intervention, 1*(1), 94.

Behavior problems are increasing in frequency among preschool children. Thus, preschool teachers must be prepared to manage the increasing disruptive behaviors exhibited in their classrooms. Because positive behavioral management strategies are accepted by teachers and have been proven effective, token economies may be promising interventions to manage disruptive behavior in the classroom. However, little research has been conducted in this area. In addition, there are developmental, practical, and philosophical issues that should be considered before token economies are recommended for preschool classrooms. This paper reviews the relevant research in this area and addresses each of these concerns. (PsycINFO Database Record (c) 2014 APA, all rights reserved)

Filcheck, H. A., McNeil, C. B., Greco, L. A., & Bernard, R. S. (2004). Using a whole-class token economy and coaching of teacher skills in a preschool classroom to manage disruptive behavior. *Psychology in the Schools, 41*, 351–361. doi:10.1002/pits.10168

The level system is a whole-classroom approach for managing disruptive behavior that employs behavioral management strategies such as a token economy, response cost, stimulating rewards, and strategic attention. Using an ABACC' treatment comparison design with follow-up, this study evaluates the effectiveness of the level system in a preschool classroom compared to (a) strategies already employed by the teacher; and (b) coaching the teacher in the Child-Directed Interaction (CDI) and Parent-Directed Interaction (PDI) phases of Parent–Child Interaction Therapy (PCIT). Teacher- and parent-report measures were administered, and behavioral observation data were collected for child and teacher behavior using videotapes. Results suggest that the amount of inappropriate behavior exhibited by children decreased when the level system was implemented. Additionally, inappropriate behavior decreased further during the CDI and PDI conditions. © 2004 Wiley Periodicals, Inc. Psychol Schs 41: 351–361, 2004.

Fjellstedt, N., & Sulzer-Azaroff, B. (1973). Reducing the latency of a child's responding to instructions by means of a token system. *Journal of Applied Behavior Analysis, 6*, 125–130.

The response latency of following directions by an eight-year-old boy from a class for emotionally disturbed children is modified by the contingent application of a token system. To demonstrate reinforcer effectiveness, a multiple baseline approach was used. Measures were obtained for the time elapsed between the presentation of verbal directions and five performances: (1) entering the experimental room; (2) putting toys away; (3) beginning academic work; (4) putting toys away again; and (5) returning to the classroom and completing preparations for leaving school. These five measures were placed on the token system at three different times. The results demonstrate that four of the five performances were clearly affected by the token system as their response latency for following directions decreased substantially.

Girardeau, F. L., & Spradlin, J. E. (1964). Token rewards in a cottage program. *Mental Retardation, 2,* 345–351.

> A program based on positive reinforcement is established to manage and train moderately and severely retarded girls in a residential center. Tokens were established as generalized reinforcers by making them redeemable in foods, soft drinks, jewelry, clothing, and novelties. These tokens were delivered to the children whenever they were engaged in constructive socially acceptable activities. Socially acceptable behavior appeared to increase in frequency. (PsycINFO Database Record (c) 2012 APA, all rights reserved)

Glynn, S. M. (1990). Token economy approaches for psychiatric patients'progress and pitfalls over 25 years. *Behavior Modification, 14*(4), 383–407.

> Although the token economy is among the most well-validated and effective behavioral treatments for schizophrenia and other serious psychiatric disorders, its use in clinical and research settings has declined from a peak in the early 1970s. Reasons for this decrease in use include staff resistance, reduced length of inpatient admissions, greater emphasis on community-based treatments, economic constraints, and legal and ethical challenges. Nevertheless, a small but enthusiastic group of proponents still conducts token economy research and treatment. Important topics pertaining to the token economy remain to be addressed, including specifying its remediative components, developing strategies to promote generalization and maintenance of treatment gains, and creating better methods to identify patients who would most benefit from participating in these programs.

Green, R. L., & Stachnik, T. J. (1968). Money, motivation, and academic achievement. *Phi Delta Kappan, 50,* 228–230.

> Educators dream of "intrinsic motivation" for academic achievement, but it seems to be in short supply, particularly among disadvantaged students. In this article, two educators offer an answer so obvious that apparently no one has proposed it before: to motivate learning, let's pay such students with quick, hard cash.

Greene, D., Sternberg, B., & Lepper, M. R. (1976). Overjustification in a token economy. *Journal of Personality and Social Psychology 34*(6), 1219–1234. doi:10.1037/0022-3514.34.6.1219

Designed a classroom token economy to discover whether demonstrably effective reinforcement procedures would also produce an overjustification effect, indicated by a significant decrement in post-treatment engagement with previously reinforced activities, in the absence of perceived tangible or social rewards. Three different experimental token economy groups formed with 33 fourth- and fifth-graders are compared with a single control group of 11 subjects. Following baseline observations, a treatment phase was initiated, during which differential reinforcement was made contingent on time spent with designated "target" activities. During this phase, subjects in all three experimental groups spent significantly more time with these activities than did the nondifferentially reinforced controls. Subsequently, after differential reinforcement was withdrawn, subjects in two of the three experimental groups spent significantly less time with their target activities than controls did, demonstrating that multiple-trial contingent reinforcement procedures are capable of producing overjustification effects. The relationship between these findings and the problem of achieving generalization of treatment effects from token economies is discussed. (49 ref) (PsycINFO Database Record (c) 2012 APA, all rights reserved)

Gresham, F. M. (1979). Comparison of response cost and time-out in a special education setting. *Journal of Special Education, 13*, 199–208. doi:10.1177/002246697901300211

Two punishment procedures, response cost and time-out, are compared to determine their effectiveness in reducing rates of noncompliance in a class of educable mentally retarded children. Response cost consisted of taking tokens away from a child contingent upon noncompliance with teacher commands. Time-out consisted of placing noncompliant children outside of the group for one minute for each noncompliance. Results suggest that response cost was as effective as the response-cost-plus-time-out contingency and that it was the controlling variable in the reduction of noncompliant behavior. The potential of response cost as an effective alternative to the use of time-out is discussed, and ethical and legal ramifications concerning the use of punishment in special education settings are addressed.

Gripp, R. F., & Magaro, P. A. (1971). A token economy program evaluation with untreated control ward comparisons. *Behavior Research and Therapy, 9,* 137–149.

> Schizophrenic patients in a token economy program residing on one ward in a state hospital are compared with control patients on other wards on a number of behavior-rating scales. Results indicate an overall decrease in those scale factors most associated with psychotic behavior. The paper also suggests a means to shorten the time required to establish the effectiveness of the reinforcement contingencies in a token program.

Heitzman, A. J. (1970). Effects of a token reinforcement system on the reading and arithmetic skills learnings of migrant primary school pupils. *Journal of Educational Research, 63,* 455–458.

> The New York State Center for Migrant Studies conducted this 1968 study, which investigated effects of token reinforcers on reading and arithmetic skills learnings of migrant primary school students during a six-week summer school session. Students (black and Caucasian) received plastic tokens to reward skills learning responses. Tokens were traded for candy, toys, or sundries to provide supplementary reinforcement. Treatment groups (n=30) were compared with nontreatment groups (n = 30) by means of at-test using scores of the Wide Range Achievement Test. Pretest and posttest comparisons favor the treatment group at the .05 level. Four tables give data relative to the study. (AN)

Henchy, V. (2012). Use of token reinforcement as a means of improving the self-help skills of a group of trainable retarded children. *Graduate Research in Education and Related Disciplines, 5,* 124–136.

> The task is learning to tie a shoelace. A prosthetic training device constructed by E was used. Twelve 8.4- to11.3-year-old subjects were selected from special classes in a day elementary school and were matched on the basis of IQ, age, sex, etc. Six experimental subjects received M&M candies for each successful attempt. Training periods were 15 minutes for each of 15 days. Training consisted of three phases: imitation, elimination of imitation and introduction of verbal instruction, and independent tying without assistance. The difference in mean number of days

to reach the second phase was not significant (p>.05). There was no difference in mean number of days to reach the last phase (p > .05). (PsycINFO Database Record (c) 2012 APA, all rights reserved)

Hermann, J. A., DeMontes, A. I., Dominguez, B., Montes, F., & Hopkins, B. L. (1973). Effects of bonuses for punctuality on the tardiness of industrial workers. *Journal of Applied Behavior Analysis, 6,* 563–570.

This study evaluates the effectiveness of an incentive procedure designed to increase the punctuality of six workers who were chronically late to work in a manufacturing company. The six workers in the experiment received a bonus of 2.00 pesos (US$0.16) for every day that they arrived on time. A reversal design was used. The contingent bonuses increased the workers'rates of punctuality compared to their baseline rates. A control group of six workers observed during the same 77-week period showed a trend toward decreasing punctuality. These results suggest that the use of small daily bonuses is a practical procedure for modifying chronic tardiness among industrial workers.

Higgins, J. W., Williams, R. L., & McLaughlin, T. F. (2001). The effects of a token economy employing instructional consequences for a third-grade student with learning disabilities: A data-based case study. *Education & Treatment of Children, 24,* 99–106.

The purpose of this investigation was to determine if a token reinforcement program could decrease three inappropriate behaviors (out of seat, talking out, and poor posture) of an elementary student with learning disabilities. The effects of the token program were examined using a multiple baseline design across behaviors. The results indicate that awarding tokens for the absence of the three target behaviors is an effective procedure. The practical aspects of the token program, as well as the difficulties of employing data collection in an integrated elementary classroom setting, are discussed.

Hillman, B. W. (1970). The effect of knowledge of results and token reinforcement on arithmetic achievement of elementary school children. *Arithmetic Teacher, 17,* 676–682.

Arithmetic achievement of fifth grade students is investigated under three treatments: immediate knowledge of results, immediate knowledge with token reinforcement, and delayed (24 hours) knowledge with no reinforcement. Differences between treatment groups were not significant. (RS)

Holt, M. M., Hobbs, T. R., & Hankins, R. (1976). The effects of token reinforcement on delinquents'classroom behavior. *Psychology in the Schools, 13*(3), 341–347.

The effects of a token reinforcement program on the classroom behavior of 19 delinquent boys in a correctional institution were investigated. Appropriate classroom behavior was defined in terms of four component categories: on-time/in-seat, on-task, social interaction, and assignment completion. A measure of total appropriate classroom behavior was calculated by summing the frequency of target response occurrence for each component behavior. Withdrawal and reinstatement of token reinforcement procedures demonstrated experimental control of total appropriate classroom behavior; however, considerable variability of component behaviors was observed. Token reinforcement control was most clearly demonstrated with on-time/in-seat behavior; assignment behavior was similarly influenced but showed greater variability; on-task behavior was noticeably affected, but exhibited an ascending trend during the reversal phase; and social interaction behavior showed fluctuations that appeared unrelated to reinforcement contingencies. These findings suggest that the use of global, composite measures may mask program effects on important component behaviors.

Hundert, J., & Batstone, D. (1978). A practical procedure to maintain pupils'accurate self-rating in a classroom token program. *Behavior Modification, 2*(1), 93–112. doi:10.1177/014544557821006

Hunt, J. G., & Zimmerman, J. (1969). Stimulating productivity in a simulated sheltered workshop setting. *American Journal of Mental Deficiency, 74*, 43–49.

Examines productivity in "exit word" patients participating in a simulated workshop setting as a function of introducing a bonus pay procedure. Work units completed/hour served as the dependent variable, and coupons redeemable for canteen items served as reinforcers. The bonus procedure: (1) significantly increased group productivity above that previously obtained under non-bonus conditions; and (2) differentially maintained productivity at values consistently higher than those obtained during temporally adjacent non-bonus periods. Results can be accounted for on the basis of the bonus procedure, influenced by verbal instructions given in conjunction with that procedure. (PsycINFO Database Record (c) 2012 APA, all rights reserved)

Ingham, R. J., & Andrews, G. (1973). An analysis of a token economy in stuttering therapy. *Journal of Applied Behavior Analysis, 6,* 219–229.

A stuttering therapy program in which adult stutterers were hospitalized and treated in small groups (n = 4) under token economy conditions is described. The token system reinforced reductions and penalized increases in stuttering during conversation. The therapy program was divided into three stages. Initially, subjects were treated by the token system, which was then integrated with a delayed auditory feedback schedule designed to instate and shape a prolonged speech pattern into normal fluent speech. Finally, subjects passed through a speech situation hierarchy while under token control conditions. Experiments conducted in the first two stages of treatment are described. The first-stage experiments examined the design of the token system; the second-stage experiment assessed the effect of a contingent punishment schedule integrated with the delayed auditory feedback procedure in order to shape rate of speaking as well as fluency.

Inkster, J. A., & McLaughlin, T. F. (1993). Token reinforcement: Effects for reducing tardiness with a socially disadvantaged adolescent student. *BC Journal of Special Education, 17*(3), 284–288.

This study found that microcomputer free time was a very effective consequence in decreasing the tardiness of a middle school boy, in improving his academic achievement, and in improving the student's attitude toward school and school assignments. (Author/JDD)

Iwata, B. A., & Bailey, J. S. (1974). Reward versus cost token systems: An analysis of the effects on students and teacher. *Journal of Applied Behavior Analysis, 7,* 567–576.

The effects of reward and cost token procedures on the social and academic behavior of two groups of elementary special-education students are assessed using a reversal design. Behavioral observations of three target subjects in each group revealed that both procedures were about equally effective in reducing rule violations and off-task behavior. Records kept on the daily arithmetic performance of all subjects showed that output doubled in both groups during the token phases, although accuracy remained unchanged. When students were allowed to choose either contingency, no pattern of preference was established. Small differences were found in teacher behavior: the reward procedure led to an increase in approval comments, but cost procedures produced no changes in teacher behavior.

Kazdin, A. E. (1971). Toward a client-administered token reinforcement program. *Education and Training of the Mentally Retarded, 6,* 52–55.

A behavior modification program in a sheltered workshop is discussed. Within the context of an operant conditioning (token economy) program, procedures are discussed that use the clients themselves to administer the reinforcement contingencies of other clients. Case material is presented, which suggests that client-administered contingencies, if properly monitored, may have some advantages over staff-administered contingencies.

Kazdin, A. E. (1971). The effect of response cost in suppressing behavior in a pre-psychotic retardate. *Journal of Behavior Therapy and Experimental Psychiatry, 2,* 137–140. doi:10.1016/0005-7916(71)90029-2

The present report describes the use of response cost (withdrawal of tokens) to suppress behavior in a pre-psychotic retarded client in a sheltered workshop setting. The 29-year-old female subject had a long-standing problem of emitting psychotic verbalizations. Her participation in a token program had improved her work-oriented behaviors without affecting these verbalizations. The response cost contingency, which was carried out by the client's supervisor for six weeks, involved the removal of tokens whenever the target behavior was performed. The treatment was effective in virtually eliminating the emitted statements.

A follow-up conducted weekly for four weeks after the contingency had been terminated showed that the behavior continued to decline and was effectively eliminated.

Kazdin, A. E. (1972).   Response cost: The removal of conditioned reinforcers for therapeutic change. *Behavior Therapy, 3*, 533–546.

Response cost (RC), a punishment procedure in which conditioned reinforcers (points, tokens, or money) are withdrawn to suppress a response, has been used as a behavior therapy technique on its own and in conjunction with reinforcement in token economies. Studies in both laboratory and clinical settings are reviewed. The following conclusions are made: (1) RC has suppressed a variety of behaviors (e.g., smoking, overeating, stuttering, psychotic talk) with diverse clinical populations (e.g., psychotics, sociopaths, retardates, school children); (2) behaviors suppressed with RC often do not recover when the punishment contingency is withdrawn; and (3) undesirable side effects frequently associated with punishment typically are not found with RC. The paucity of studies with long-term follow-up periods and careful examination of side effects makes the last two conclusions tentative. Aspects of RC which may contribute to its efficacy are discussed. These include cost magnitude, instructions, and informative feedback. Recommendations are made for increased use of RC as a behavior therapy technique.

Kazdin, A. E. (1973). The effect of vicarious reinforcement on attentive behavior in the classroom. *Journal of Applied Behavior Analysis, 6*, 71–78.

The effect of social reinforcement delivered to target subjects on the attentive behavior of adjacent peers is examined in a classroom setting. In a combined reversal and multiple baseline design, two pairs of mentally retarded children were sequentially exposed to three reinforcement phases. After baseline rates of attentive behavior were obtained, praise was delivered to the target subject in each subject pair for attentive behavior. After a reversal phase, praise was delivered contingently to target subjects for inattentive behavior. In a final phase, contingent praise for attentive behavior was reinstated for the target subjects. Throughout the study, nontarget subjects received no direct reinforcers. The results indicate a vicarious reinforcement effect. Reinforcing attentive behavior of target subjects increased this behavior in adjacent peers. However, reinforcing INATTENTIVE behavior of target subjects also increased the ATTENTIVE behavior of adjacent peers. The effects obtained through vicarious reinforcement were considered to reflect the discriminative stimulus properties of reinforcement, which may serve as a cue for the performance of non-reinforced peers.

Kazdin, A. E. (1975). *Behavior modification in applied settings.* Homewood, IL: Dorsey.

Kazdin, A. E. (1977). *The token economy: A review and evaluation.* New York: Plenum Press.

Kazdin, A. E. (1982). The token economy: A decade later. *Journal of Applied Behavior Analysis, 15*(3), 431–445.

In the last decade, the token economy has been extended widely across populations and behaviors in treatment, rehabilitation, educational, and community settings. Outcome research has expanded as well to include large-scale program evaluations and comparative and combined treatment studies of the token economy. In a previous review (Kazdin & Bootzin, 1972), several obstacles were identified for the effective application of the token economy. These included identifying procedures to enhance program efficacy, to train staff, to overcome client resistance, and to promote long-term maintenance and transfer of training. The present paper discusses recent advances in research and reviews progress on the major issues identified previously. New issues have become salient in the last decade that pertain to the extension of the token economy to institutional settings. The demands for maintaining the integrity of treatment, the ability to integrate token economies within existing institutional constraints, and the disseminability of the procedures on a large scale are major issues that may dictate the future of the token economy.

Kazdin, A. E., & Bootzin, R. R. (1972). The token economy: An evaluative review. *Journal of Applied Behavior Analysis, 5*, 343–372. doi:10.1901/jaba.1972.5-343

Token economies have been applied in a wide range of settings. While there are several advantages to the use of this procedure, there are obstacles that may impede its implementation and therapeutic efficacy. These include: staff training, client resistance, circumvention of the contingencies, and nonresponsiveness of subjects. Studies employing token programs with psychiatric patients, retardates, children in classroom settings, delinquents, and autistic children are reviewed. Although token economies are successful while in operation, the issue of generalization of behavior gains or resistance to extinction has not been given careful consideration. Inasmuch as generalization is perhaps the most crucial issue, several procedures are presented that are designed to facilitate maintenance of performance when reinforcement is withdrawn. Methodological suggestions for investigations on token reinforcement in applied settings are presented.

Kazdin, A. E., & Geesey, S. (1980). Enhancing classroom attentiveness by preselection of back reinforcers in a token economy. *Behavior Modification, 4*, 98–114.

Kazdin, A. E., & Mascitelli, S. (1980). The opportunity to earn oneself off a token system as a reinforcer for attentive behavior. *Behavior Therapy, 11*, 68–78.

Separate token reinforcement contingencies are compared with two mentally retarded children in a special education classroom. Each child receives tokens contingent upon attentive behavior while working on academic tasks. The separate contingencies consist of providing the children with token reinforcement that includes the opportunity to earn their way off the system versus a similar contingency that does not provide this opportunity. The two contingencies were compared in separate simultaneous-treatment designs for each child. The contingencies were implemented daily and were balanced across different time periods. Providing children with the opportunity to earn their way off the system led to higher levels of attentive behavior than did the contingency without this added backup event. The results suggest that opportunities to earn one's way off the system can reinforce behavior and perhaps provide an initial step in weaning clients from a highly structured reinforcement program.

Kerr, M. M., & Nelson, C. M. (1998). *Strategies for managing behavior problems in the classroom* (3rd ed.). Upper Saddle River, NJ: Merrill.
Klimas, A., & McLaughlin, T. F. (2007). The effects of a token economy system to improve social and academic behavior with a rural primary-aged child with disabilities. *International Journal of Special Education, 22*(3).

The purpose of the present case report was to evaluate the effects of an individual token economy with a young child with severe behavior disorders. Three behaviors were recorded: time to completion; the number of assignments completed; and the frequency of inappropriate behavior. These data were gathered for 30 minutes each morning. The overall outcomes indicate that the two different token systems were effective in improving the participant's academic and social behavior. The amount of work that was required could be increased without a large decrement in academic output or increases in inappropriate behavior. The program was enjoyed by both the teaching staff and the participant. Suggestions for future research and the maintenance of treatment gains are made.

Knapczyk, D. R., & Livingston, G. (1973). Self-recording and student teacher supervision: Variables within a token economy structure. *Journal of Applied Behavior Analysis, 6,* 481–486.

A token system is used to attempt to increase the accuracy with which special education students answer questions about reading assignments. In the token system, students record their own data, receive toy money for accurately completing assignments, and are allowed to spend their toy money at the end of the week for educational activities. The accuracy with which students answered questions was higher when the token system was in effect than when it was not. When student teachers were used to manage the token system and when the self-recording feature of the system was removed, only slight changes in the accuracy of the student performance were obtained.

Kohn, A. (1999). *Punished by rewards: The trouble with gold stars, incentive plans, A's, praise, and other bribes.* New York: Houghton Mifflin.

Kuypers, D. S., Becker, W. C., & O'Leary, K. D. (1968). How to make a token system fail. *Exceptional Children, 35(2),* 101–109.

A token system is instituted in an adjustment class of six third- and fourth-graders. The aim of the study was to examine aspects of token systems critical in making them effective. The results indicate a significant degree of improvement in behavior attributable to the token program, but when compared to the highly effective program reported by O'Leary and Becker (1967), it is apparent that an effective program requires more than tokens and backup reinforcers.

Lehrer, P., Schiff, L., & Kris, A. (1970). The use of a credit card in a token economy. *Journal of Applied Behavior Analysis, 3*, 289–291.

No abstract is available for this article.

Lloyd, K. E., & Abel, L. (1970). Performance on a token economy psychiatric ward: A two-year summary. *Behavior Research and Therapy, 8*, 1–9.

A token economy psychiatric hospital ward for chronic schizophrenic male and female patients is described in detail. After two years, 13 patients had been discharged; 6 were hospital employees, 12 had earned many privileges on the token ward, 12 had earned very few privileges, and 9 had been removed from the ward. The patients in these five terminal positions were compared on age, years-in-hospital, prescribed drugs, and diagnosis. The median years-in-hospital for discharged patients was lower than the median for the other four terminal positions. Otherwise, comparisons of these variables revealed no consistent trends. The proportion of time the patients spent out of the hospital was greater after entering the token ward than before entering it. The two-thirds of patient movements from one of the five positions to another were in the direction of improvement of socially acceptable behavior.

Lloyd, K., Ed., & Garlington, W. K. (1968). Weekly variations in performance on a token economy psychiatric ward. *Behavior Research and Therapy, 6*, 407–410.

Seven types of behavior of 13 chronic schizophrenic female patients, who were transferred to an existing male token economy ward, are rated during four experimental phases. During Conditions I and III, the patients were given a token allowance in the morning on a noncontingent basis. During Conditions II and IV, tokens were paid on a contingent basis; that is, the patients received tokens commensurate with their behavior ratings. Their ratings were higher during Conditions II and IV than during Conditions I and III. The results support the expectation that the contingent tokens were controlling the behavior of the patients.

Macdonald, M. A., & Sherman, P. D. (1987). Stuck for words: Combining social skills training with a token economy system for adolescents. *Journal of Child Care, 3*(1), 51–58.

Describes an approach designed to increase social-skill generalization by combining a structured social-skills-training (SST) package with an achievement-place-type of residential token economy program. Six adolescents from the residences and day treatment programs were involved in a coed SST group. The residential subjects received further reinforcement of training via individual programs within the residential setting. The training experience is discussed with respect to generalization, the feasibility of the SST package, and its usefulness. (PsycINFO Database Record (c) 2012 APA, all rights reserved)

Maggin, D. M., Chafouleas, S. M., Goddard, K. M., & Johnson, A. H. (2011). A systematic evaluation of token economies as a classroom management tool for students with challenging behavior. *Journal of School Psychology, 49*(5), 529–554.

A two-part systematic review is undertaken to assess the effectiveness of token economies in increasing rates of appropriate classroom behavior for students demonstrating behavioral difficulties. The first part of the review employs the recently published What Works Clearinghouse (WWC) standards for evaluating single-subject research to determine the extent to which eligible studies demonstrated sufficient evidence to classify the token economy as an evidence-based practice. The second part of the review employs meta-analytic techniques across four different types of effect sizes to evaluate the quantitative strength of the findings. Methodological strengths and weaknesses across the studies were systematically investigated. Results indicate that the extant research on token economies does not provide sufficient evidence to be deemed best practice based on the WWC criteria.

Maglio, C., & McLaughlin, T. F. (1981). Effects of a token reinforcement system and teacher attention in reducing inappropriate verbalization with a junior high school student. *Corrective and Social Psychiatry, 27,* 140–145.

Token reinforcement and teacher attention are successful in reducing inappropriate verbalizations in a 14-year-old female; this reduction is also maintained over fading and follow-up periods. (29 ref) (PsycINFO Database Record (c) 2012 APA, all rights reserved)

Mandelker, A. V., Brigham, T. A., & Bushell, D. (1970). The effects of token procedures on a teacher's social contacts with her students. *Journal of Applied Behavior Analysis, 3*, 169–174.

> The effects of a token system on a teacher's rate of social contacts with her students are investigated in a public school kindergarten. A group of six children were observed daily during a 20-minute handwriting lesson. The children were divided into two groups (A and B) of three children each. Five conditions were imposed sequentially: (1) baseline without tokens; (2) contingent tokens for Group A, noncontingent tokens for Group B; (3) contingent tokens for Group B, noncontingent tokens for Group A; (4) reinstatement of condition 2; and (5) contingent tokens for both groups. It was consistently observed that the teacher's rate of social contact was higher with the children receiving the contingent tokens than with those who received noncontingent tokens.

Matson, J. L., & Boisjoli, J. A. (2009). The token economy for children with intellectual disability and/or autism: A review. *Research on Developmental Disabilities, 30*, 240–248. doi:10.1016/j.ridd.2008.04.001

> One of the most important technologies of behavior modifiers and applied behavior analysts over the last 40 years has been the token economy. These procedures are useful in that they help provide a structured therapeutic environment and mimic other naturally occurring reinforcement systems such as the use of money. Token economies, at least from a research standpoint, appeared to have crested in popularity during the 1980s. However, for children with intellectual disability (ID) and/or autism, such methods continue to hold considerable therapeutic promise. An overview of past developments, current status, and potential future trends and applications with respect to this special population is presented.

McGinnis, C. J., Friman, P. C., & Carlyon, W. D. (1999). The effect of token awards on "intrinsic" motivation for doing math. *Journal of Applied Behavior Analysis, 32*(3), 375–379.

> A multielement baseline design is used to analyze effects of token rewards delivered contingent upon completion of math problems by two middle-school boys. Time spent on math and amount of math completed increased during reward

conditions and were maintained during fading and withdrawal. At follow-up, results were maintained for one boy, but fell below baseline for the other. (Author/DB)

McGoey, K. E., & DuPaul, G. J. (2000). Token Reinforcement and Response Cost Procedures: Reducing the Disruptive Behavior of Preschool Children with Attention-Deficit/Hyperactivity Disorder. *School Psychology Quarterly, 15*, 330–343.

Compares the effects of a token reinforcement and a response cost intervention in reducing the disruptive behavior of four preschool children with attention-deficit/hyperactivity disorder. Results show that both interventions were effective; teachers rated both highly acceptable with a preference for response cost. Implications for future research and practice are discussed. (Author/MKA)

McKenzie, H. S., Clark, M., Wolf, M., Kothera, R., & Benson, C. (1968). Behavior modification of children with learning disabilities using grades as tokens and allowances as backup reinforcers. *Exceptional Children, 34*, 745–752.

The modification of academic behaviors of children in a learning disabilities class was undertaken by arranging for events such as amount of teacher attention, recess, and quality of weekly grade reports to be consequences for academic progress. As academic behaviors achieved with these consequences stabilized at less than an optimal level, the children's parents agreed to have the children earn their allowances on the basis of the weekly grade reports. This token reinforcement system, with grades as tokens and with allowances as added backup reinforcers, significantly increased the children's academic behaviors. (PsycINFO Database Record (c) 2013 APA, all rights reserved)

McLaughlin, T. F. (1975). The applicability of token reinforcement systems in public school systems. *Psychology in the Schools.*

Reviews token reinforcement programs that have been conducted in public schools. Programs are examined in terms of (a) effectiveness; (b) ease of implementation and management; (c) expense; (d) compatibility with school and

McLaughlin, T. F., & Malaby, J. (1972). Intrinsic reinforcers in a classroom token economy. *Journal of Applied Behavior Analysis, 5*, 263–270.

An inexpensive, easily managed token economy is used in a normal classroom for one academic year, and data are collected for the entire academic performance in spelling, language, handwriting, and math for that year. During a baseline period, assignment completion was variable. The introduction of a token economy with a point exchange every five days increased assignment completion and decreased variability of performance. An application of a token economy that had a point exchange averaging four days was accompanied by an assignment completion rate that approximated 100 percent. A reinforcement contingency for which quiet behavior rather than for assignment completion was eased; quiet behavior was accompanied by a marked diminution of assignment completion. A reintroduction of the token reinforcement for assignment completion system increased assignment completion again.

McLaughlin, T. F., & Williams, R. L. (1988). The token economy in the classroom. In J. C. Witt, S. N. Elliott, & F. M. Gresham (Eds.). *Handbook of behavior therapy in education* (pp. 469–487). New York: Plenum.

Miller, L. K., & Schneider, R. (1970). The use of a token system in Project Head Start. *Journal of Applied Behavior Analysis, 3*, 213–220.

The present experiment sought to develop a practical and effective method for teaching the beginning elements of handwriting in a Head Start program. The method consisted of reinforcing responses to a writing program by giving the children access to a variety of activities normally available in the preschool classroom. Tokens were presented for correct responses. The children then used the tokens to select reinforcers such as snacks and access to a variety of play activities. In an experimental evaluation of the token system, it was found that responding was maintained as long as access to the reinforcing activities was contingent upon responding. When reinforcement was no longer contingent upon responding, virtually no responding occurred. Informal observations suggested that the token system had several unanticipated effects: the children's vocabulary and ability to understand instructions improved; a favorable attitude toward school developed; and their ability to play cooperatively with other children increased. It was concluded that the token system is a practical and effective method for teaching beginning writing skills and that it has other desirable, if unanticipated, effects.

Music, J. K., & Luckey, R. E. (1970). Program Profiles: A Token Economy for Moderately and Severely Retarded. *Mental Retardation, 8*, 35–36.

To improve the behavior of those moderately and severely retarded no longer attending classes, a token economy was established at Denton State School. Data are reported on 60 male residents aged 17 to 30 years old who were initially placed on a token economy. Good behavior was rewarded with social and recreational privileges. Prior to the one-year study, subjects frequently complained of illness and exhibited unruly behavior. At its conclusion, subjects occupied their time constructively, performing chores, attending to personal grooming, and cooperating with superiors. Undesirable behavior and reports of sickness had decreased. Employees gained new respect for their charges and were eager to provide them with enjoyable activities. (PsycINFO Database Record (c) 2012 APA, all rights reserved)

Naughton, C. C., & McLaughlin, T. F. (1995). The use of a token economy system for students with behaviour disorders. *BC Journal of Special Education, 19*, 29–38.

This paper discusses how to set up and implement a token economy system for students with behavior disorders in a classroom setting. The available literature is reviewed, and it is concluded that token economies have been proven effective in improving behavior among students with social and academic deficits. (Author/PB)

O'Hara, E. A. (1970). Using pay to change mentally retarded students' work behavior. *Teaching Exceptional Children, 2*, 163–169.

No abstract is available for this article.

O'Leary, K. D., & Becker, W. C. (1967). Behavior modification of an adjustment class: A token reinforcement program. *Exceptional Children, 33 (9),* 637–642.

A base rate of deviant behavior is obtained for the eight most disruptive children in a third-grade adjustment class. In a token reinforcement program, the children received teacher's ratings, which were exchangeable for reinforcers such as candy and trinkets. With the introduction of the token reinforcement program, an abrupt reduction in deviant behavior occurred. Delay of reinforcement was gradually increased to four days without increase in deviant behavior. The program was equally successful for all children observed, and anecdotal evidence suggests that the children's appropriate behavior generalized to other school situations. (Author)

O'Leary, K. D., Becker, W. C., Evans, M. B., & Saudargas, R. A. (1969). A token reinforcement program in a public school: A replication and systematic analysis. *Journal of Applied Behavior Analysis, 2,* 3–13.

No abstract is available for this article.

O'Leary, K. D., & Drabman, R. (1971). Token reinforcement programs in the classroom: A review. *Psychological Bulletin, 75,* 379–398.

Examines a number of factors which may critically influence the success of a token program, including the teacher, the child, the parent, and the system of reinforcement. Methodological considerations (e.g., type of experimental design, bias, and replicability) are discussed. Several methodological problems in token reinforcement studies are noted. A number of suggestions are presented for the assessmentofthelong-termeffectivenessoftokenreinforcementprograms.(2P.Ref.) (PsycINFO Database Record (c) 2012 APA, all rights reserved)

Phillips, E. L. (1968). Achievement place: Token reinforcement procedures in a home-style rehabilitation setting for "pre-delinquent" boys. *Journal of Applied Behavior Analysis, 1(3),* 213–223.

Token reinforcement procedures are designed to modify the behavior of "pre-delinquent" boys residing in a community-based, home-style rehabilitation setting. Points (the tokens) were redeemable for various privileges such as visiting their families, watching TV, and riding bicycles. Points were given by the house-parents, contingent upon specified appropriate behavior and taken away for specified inappropriate behavior. The frequencies of aggressive statements and poor grammar decreased, while tidiness, punctuality, and amount of homework completed increased. It is concluded that a token reinforcement procedure, entirely dependent upon back-up reinforcers naturally available in a home-style treatment setting, could contribute to an effective and economical rehabilitation program for pre-delinquents.

Phillips, E. L., Phillips, E. A., Fixsen, D. L., & Wolf, M. M. (1971). Achievement place: Modification of the behaviors of pre-delinquent boys within a token economy. *Journal of Applied Behavior Analysis, 4*, 45–50. doi:10.1901/jaba.1971.4-45

Piper, T. (1972). A token reinforcement procedure in a third grade inner city classroom. *Education, 92*(3), 18–22.

   Advantages of the system described include the minimal cost, the simplicity of operation and minimal training required, the change in classroom atmosphere from negative-defensive to positive-receptive, and the opportunity to teach arithmetic and money skills. (Authors)

Rapport, M. D., Murphy, A., & Bailey, J. S. (1980). The effects of a response cost treatment tactic on hyperactive children. *Journal of School Psychology, 18*, 98–111. doi:10.1016/0022-4405(80)90025-4

   Testing of a response cost procedure, compared with Ritalin treatment, on hyperactive elementary school children to determine effectiveness in reducing hyperactive behavior and in increasing academic performance. The cost program alone, combined with medication, was effective in reducing off-task behavior and in increasing academic performance. (Author/BEF)

Reitman, D., Murphy, M. A., Hupp, S. D. A., & O'Callaghan, P. M. (2004). Behavior change and perceptions of change: Evaluating the effectiveness of a token economy. *Child & Family Behavior Therapy, 26*(2), 17–36. doi:10.1300/J019v26n02 02

Token economies often reduce problematic classroom behavior in preschool settings. In the present study, direct observation and teacher ratings of child behavior and treatment acceptability are employed to evaluate the effectiveness of a token economy in a Head Start classroom. Because many teachers express concerns about the effort required to implement and maintain token systems, this study compares the relative efficacies of group and individualized contingency management programs. Direct observation data for three children reveal that both the individual and group contingency were superior to a baseline condition in which no systematic behavior management program was employed. In addition, the whole group contingency was generally as effective as the individual contingency. However, despite reductions in classroom rule violations for the three target children, the acceptability of the token program was variable, and little change was observed in the teacher's ratings of their behavior. The results suggest the ongoing need for multiple measures of treatment outcome (e.g., teacher and student ratings of acceptability and effectiveness; direct observation) even for empirically supported school-based interventions.

Ringer, V. M. J. (1973). The use of a "token helper" in the management of classroom behavior problems and in teacher training. *Journal of Applied Behavior Analysis, 6*(4), 671–677.

A grade-four class teacher is trained in the use of token and verbal reinforcement by an experienced "token helper," who demonstrates the procedures in the classroom. The introduction of a simple token system resulted in significant decreases in the disruptive behavior of ten pupils in two morning periods. When the token helper withdrew from the classroom, the teacher managed the token system and maintained disruptive behavior at lower-than-baseline levels.

Roberts, C. L., & Perry, R. M. (1970). A total token economy. *Mental Retardation, 8*, 15–18.

Describes a program of behavior modification using principles derived from the experimental analysis of behavior being implemented for the entire population of the Mental Retardation Center in Pueblo, Colorado. The goals, general procedures, and problems encountered are discussed. Since the program is designed both to include all residents and personnel in a systematic effort and to rely heavily on generalized reinforcers (e.g., tokens), the program is considered to be a total token economy. The position is taken that the available evidence indicates operant-conditioning principles constitute the major method of choice for the improvement of the behavior of retardates. The essential task of those who work with retardates is considered to be teaching. (15 ref.) (PsycINFO Database Record (c) 2012 APA, all rights reserved)

Ruskin, R. S., & Maley, R. F. (1972). Item preference in a token economy ward store. *Journal of Applied Behavior Analysis, 5*, 373–378.

Token spending by 20 schizophrenic patients is monitored over a six-month period. It was found that: (1) token expenditures for cigarettes and "edibles" far surpassed other store item categories; and (2) percentage increases in token expenditures were greatest for categories of items relating to appearance and grooming, strongly suggesting that store purchasing patterns over time may provide an index of program effectiveness.

Salend, S. J., & Allen, E. M. (1985). Comparative Effects of Externally Managed and Self-Managed Response-Cost Systems on Inappropriate Classroom Behavior. *Journal of School Psychology, 23*, 59–67.

This study compares the relative efficacy of externally managed and self- managed free token response cost systems in decreasing the inappropriate behavior of two learning-disabled students. The differential effects of the two treatment conditions were assessed by using an alternating treatments design. Experimental control was demonstrated by adding reversal phases comparing the treatments with baseline conditions. The results indicate that the two treatment conditions are equally effective in decreasing inappropriate behavior. The reasons for and implications of the findings are discussed.

Salend, S. J., Tintle, L., and Balber, H. (1988). Effects of a student-managed response cost system on the behavior of two mainstreamed students. *Elementary School Journal, 89*(1), 89–97.

Illustrates the use of a student-managed response cost system using free tokens to modify the on-task behavior of two mainstreamed students—an emotionally disturbed fourth-grader and a learning-disabled sixth-grader. Subjects'on-task behavior, as well as their academic performance, improved after the program. (SKC)

Sattler, H. E., & Swoope, K. S. (1970). Token systems: A procedural guide. *Psychology in the Schools, 7*, 363–384.

The authors present and discuss a ten-point guideline for the use of token systems as vehicles for the application of operant psychology to remediation of classroom problems. These procedural considerations include (1) selecting a method for choosing desirable behaviors; (2) selecting the kind of token to be awarded; (3) choosing backup reinforcers for which the tokens can be exchanged; (4) selecting a cueing method for informing children which behaviors will be reinforced; (5) choosing a mode for awarding tokens; (6) constructing a master control sheet for recording tokens awarded; (7) scheduling a time for exchanging tokens for backup reinforcers; (8) selecting a method for making backup reinforcers available; (9) devising a method for bringing the reinforcing activity period to an end; and (10) selecting the appropriate type of contingency to be used when awarding tokens.

Shook, S., LaBrie, M., Vallies, J., McLaughlin, T. F., & Williams, R. L. (1990). The effects of a token program on first-grade students'inappropriate social behavior. *Reading Improvement, 27*, 96–101.

No abstract is available for this article.

Siegel, G. M., Lenske, J., & Broen, P. (1969). Suppression of normal speech disfluencies through response cost. *Journal of Applied Behavior Analysis, 2*, 265–276.

The speech disfluencies of five normal-speaking college students are modified in a series of 10 to 17 sessions by means of response cost. During point-loss, each disfluency (repetition or interjection of a sound, syllable, word, etc.) resulted in the loss of a penny, as indicated on a screen in front of the subject. Disfluencies were suppressed and kept at very low levels for four of the subjects during the punishment procedures, and there was general resistance to extinction. Even though points were subtracted only during speech, there was a tendency for disfluencies to decrease, though not as markedly, during reading probes as well.

Sran, S. K., & Borrero, J. C. (2010). Assessing the value of choice in a token system. *Journal of Applied Behavior Analysis, 43*, 553–557.

Responding of four children is assessed under conditions in which (a) no programmed contingencies were arranged for target behavior; (b) responding produced tokens that could be exchanged for a single highly preferred edible item; and (c) responding produced a token that could be exchanged for a variety of preferred edible items. After assessing the effects of these contingencies, the preferences of three participants were assessed using a concurrent-chains schedule. Preference for the opportunity to choose from the same or qualitatively different edible items varied across participants, and findings are generally consistent with those of Tiger, Hanley, and Hernandez (2006).

Staats, A. W., Minke, K. A., & Butts, P. (1970). A token reinforcement program administered by black therapy technicians to problem black children. *Behavior Therapy, 1*, 331–353.

Reading materials in a stimulus-response presentation procedure combined with a token-reinforcement motivational system are employed with 32 black children from the ghetto in a remedial program administered by black subprofessional therapy technicians supervised by a behaviorally trained teacher. The children, who are problem learners—many considered to be emotionally disturbed, anti-social, or retarded—attended well, worked hard, and learned well in the four- to five-month program. There were two types of dependent measures: behavioral measures consisting of detailed recordings of the responses each child made, the reinforcers received, the words learned and retained and the like; and test data. The results showed the procedures and reinforcement system employed to be significantly effective in producing improved attention and work behaviors in these usually intractable children and in the employment and upgrading of unemployed black adults. However, although 40.2 hours of training was not deemed sufficient to remediate long-standing cases of educational failure, the results suggest that longer, more intensive programs of the present type could make important contributions to the solution of the social problems involved, as well as to the study of human learning.

Staats, A. W., Staats, C. K., Schutz, R. E., & Wolf, M. M. (1962). The conditioning of textual responses using "extrinsic" reinforcers. *Journal of the Experimental Analysis of Behavior, 5*, 33–40.

Six four-year-old subjects are presented with a textual program consisting of 26 words arranged so the word stimuli were gradually combined into sentences and then short "stories." Three subjects are given the No-Reinforcement condition first, and only social reinforcers were presented. They are switched to the Reinforcement condition as soon as they request discontinuance of the activity. The other three subjects are given Reinforcement-No Reinforcement-Reinforcement treatments. The No-Reinforcement treatment in this case lasted until the subject requested discontinuance of the activity. The reinforcers were mixed edibles and trinkets, as well as tokens backed up by small plastic toys on a 1:24 ratio. The unit of response was the number of new texts acquired as a result of each of the 45-minute experimental sessions. It was demonstrated that the program, procedure, and reinforcement conditions produced curves that are analogous to those produced in common operant-conditioning procedures. The results indicate that other operant principles may be studied in this significant area of human behavior, with important practical consequences.

Stilitz, I. (2009). A token economy of the early 19th century. *Journal of Applied Behavior Analysis, 42*(4), 925–926.

No abstract is available for this article.

Sullivan, M. S., & O'Leary, S. G. (1990). Maintenance following reward and cost token programs. *Behavior Therapy, 21*, 139–149.

The maintenance of treatment gains achieved in a classroom with reward and response cost token programs is compared in a group of ten children with academic and/or behavior problems. Differentially superior maintenance of on-task behavior during fading of the response cost program was predicted on the basis of differential discriminability of treatment withdrawal. A within-subjects design and analysis revealed that both the reward and response cost programs had large and equivalent treatment effects. During fading of the response cost program, all children maintained their rates of on-task behavior. During fading of the reward program, half of the children did not maintain their rates of on-task behavior, while the remaining five children did. The five non-maintainers obtained significantly elevated scores on the Aggression and Hyperactivity factors of the Teacher Rating Scale (TRS) (Conners, 1969). The results are discussed in the context of procedural differences between reward and response cost programs and theories of hyperactivity.

Swain, J. C., & McLaughlin, T. F. (1998). The Effects of Bonus Contingencies in a Classwide Token Program on Math Accuracy with Middle-School Students with Behavioral Disorders. *Behavioral Interventions, 13*, 11–19.

The effects of bonus points contingent on 80 percent accuracy in math with four middle school special education students with behavior disorders are examined. A multiple-baseline design across students was used to evaluate the effects of bonus points. The overall results indicated that higher accuracy was found for math assignments during the bonus points condition than during baseline. This overall outcome was replicated for each subject in the study. The benefits of implementing a bonus contingency within an ongoing classroom token economy with middle school students with behavior disorders are discussed. © 1998 John Wiley & Sons, Ltd.

Swiezy, N. B., Matson, J. L., & Box, P. (1993). The good behavior game: A token reinforcement system for preschoolers. *Child and Family Behavior Therapy, 14*, 21–32.

The good behavior game is implemented with four children attending a church-affiliated preschool in efforts to increase concurrent compliance and cooperation. Sessions were conducted individually with each child pair while in free play. The children were given various instructions by "Buddy Bear" (a puppet). Children were praised individually for compliant behavior, while noncompliant and inappropriate behaviors were ignored. Further instances in which children comply (i.e., cooperation) were rewarded with tokens made of felt, shaped like a happy face or dinosaur and placed on a large felt board. If the children earned their criterion levels of tokens, they received animal snacks. Improvements in compliance were noted, with generalization occurring across therapists, but not settings. Factors influencing the results and implications of the findings are discussed.

Truchlicka, M., McLaughlin, T. F., & Swain, J. C. (1998). Effects of token reinforcement and response cost on the accuracy of spelling performance with middle-school special education students with behavior disorders. *Behavioral Interventions, 13*, 1–10. doi:10.1002-(SICI)1099-078X(199802)13:1<1::AID-BINI>3.0CO;2-Z

The effects of token reinforcement and response cost on the accuracy of spelling performance with three adolescent special education students are examined. A multiple-baseline design across students was used to evaluate the effects of token reinforcement and response cost intervention. A greater percent of accuracy on daily spelling exams was obtained during the token reinforcement plus response cost condition than during the baseline condition. This was replicated for each student. Follow-up data collection indicated maintenance of behavior change over time. The benefits of implementing a token economy with a response cost component with middle school students with behavior disorders are discussed. © 1998 John Wiley & Sons, Ltd.

Tyler, V. O. (1967). Application of operant token reinforcement of academic performance of an institutionalized delinquent. *Psychological Reports, 21,* 249–260.

Operant techniques are employed to strengthen the academic performance of Nick, a glib, manipulative, delinquently identified 16-year-old boy with an IQ of 108, committed for stealing four cars. Reports stated he felt "dumb" in school and resisted the educational process. Nick "rented" the use of his mattress at night and the right to wear his clothes instead of institutional clothes and purchased canteen items (cigarettes, candy, gum, etc.) with tokens. He earned tokens with daily and weekly school grades. Over 30 weeks, average weekly grades improved slightly. Previous grade point averages were: .60, 1.-, .50, and 1.20; with reinforcement, averages rose to 3.00. Grading bias of teachers was in the opposite direction. Teachers reported Nick dislikes school, but still worked for tokens. It was concluded that token reinforcement improves academic performance, but better controlled studies are needed to develop and validate this approach.

Tyler, V. O., & Brown, G. D. (1968). Application of Operant Token Reinforcement to Academic Performance of an Institutionalized Delinquent. *Journal of Education Psychology, 59,* 164–168.

Court-committed 13- to 15-year-old boys in a training school observe a daily television newscast. The following morning in school, their teachers administer a ten-item true/false test based on program content; subjects were immediately shown their scores. After school, subjects were paid with tokens redeemable for candy, gum, etc. During phase I (17 days), Group 1 (N = 9) received tokes contingent on test performance; Group 2 (N = 6) received tokens on a noncontingent basis. During Phase II (12 days), Group 1 received noncontingent reinforcement and Group 2 contingent reinforcement. The hypothesis that test scores would be higher under contingent than noncontingent reinforcement was supported in both between- and within-subject comparisons. The conclusion is that contingent token reinforcement strengthens academic performance. (PsycINFO Database Record (c) 2012 APA, all rights reserved)

Ulmer, R. A. (1976). *On the development of a token economy mental hospital treatment program.* Washington, DC: Hemisphere Publishing Corp.

Wagner, R. F., & Guyer, B. P. (1971). Maintenance of discipline through increasing children's span of attending by means of a token economy. *Psychology in the Schools, 8,* 285–289.

> Findings suggest that conditioning a student's attending behavior to a given task seems to affect general adjustment behavior positively and thus decreases disciplinary problems in school. However, it does not seem to have an influence on performance. (Author)

Weiner, H. (1962). Some effects of response cost upon human operant behavior. *Journal of the Experimental Analysis of Behavior, 5,* 201–208.

> Three experiments are reported that investigate the effects of cost (point loss per response) upon human-observer responses maintained by VI and FI schedules of reinforcement (acquisition of points via critical-signal detections). (I) Cost-attenuated VI response rates without substantially disturbing the constancy of responding, regardless of the presentation sequence of the no-cost and cost conditions. (II) FI scalloping appeared only under cost conditions. Under no cost, a constant rate of responding (similar to VI performance) characterized inter-reinforcement intervals. Exposure to cost did not prevent the recovery of previously established no-cost baselines. (III) FI irregularities, analogous to those commonly observed under FI reinforcement schedules, may be produced by different temporal presentations of the no-cost and cost conditions.

> The results of all three experiments emphasize the importance of cost as a factor in the maintenance of human behavior on schedules of positive reinforcement.

Wexler, D. (1973). Token and taboo: Behavior modification, token economies, and the law. *California Law Review, 61,* 81–109.

> No abstract is available for this article.

Winett, R. A., Richards, C. S., Krasner, L., & Krasner, M. (1971). Child-monitored token reading program. *Psychology in the Schools, 8,* 259–262.

The author concludes that the demonstration of the effectiveness of a child-monitored token reading program in a normal classroom setting clearly indicates the feasibility of utilizing behavior modification principles for a wide range of educational endeavors. (Author)

Winkler, R. C. (1971). The relevance of economic theory and technology to token reinforcement systems. *Behavior Research and Therapy, 9,* 81–88.

The spending behaviour in a token system for chronic psychiatric patients is used to demonstrate the relevance of economic theory and technology to the understanding and planning of token systems. Spending behaviour in the token system is found to enter into relationships with patient income that are very similar to the consumption schedules and Engel curves found in economic investigations. The economic concept of the elasticity of a demand curve is shown to be applicable to patient demands in token systems. Economic theory is found to supplement reinforcement theory in the conceptualization of token system processes.

Winkler, R. C. (1973). Application of Operant Token Reinforcement to Academic Performance of an Institutionalized Delinquent. *Behavior Therapy, 4,* 22–40.

The role of savings and economic balance in a token system for chronic psychiatric patients is examined. After observation of the effects of normal changes in economic balance, savings was varied independently of economic balance in two experiments. High savings was found to produce poor performance and low savings improved performance. This savings effect was not found to be a simple function of primary deprivation level. A further three experiments found that the effect of variations in the amount of reinforcement was virtually eliminated by high savings. Savings, controlled by economic balance, was found to be a major determinant of the effectiveness of token systems.

Witt, J. C., & Elliot, S. N. (1982). The response cost lottery: A time-efficient and effective classroom intervention. *Journal of School Psychology, 20,* 155–161. doi:10.1016/0022-4405(82)90009-7

> An ABAB design was used to evaluate the effect of a response cost lottery pro-cedure on the percentage of on-task behavior and accuracy of academic work of three fourth-grade students. Although contingencies were attached primarily to behavior, both on-task behavior and academic performance measures increased in treatment conditions. Teacher reports indicate the intervention was both easy to use and effective.

Wolf, M. M., Giles, D. K., & Hall, R. V. (1968). Experiments with token reinforcement in a reme-dial classroom. *Behavior Research and Therapy, 6,* 51–64.

> This report describes results of the first year of an after-school remedial education program for low-achieving fifth- and sixth-grade children in an urban poverty area. The remedial program incorporated standard instructional materials, mastery of which was supported by token reinforcement. Experimental analyses carried out with individual students showed the token reinforcement to function as such. The effects of the program on the academic achievement and report card grades of the children in the remedial group were found to be significant when compared with the gains of a control group who had no remedial program.

Wolfe, J. B. (1936). Effectiveness of token rewards for chimpanzees. *Comparative Psychology Monograph, 11*(5, Series No. 60).

> Poker chips are found to have a reward value equivalent to food, for which, after a period of training in which they were used to obtain food from a vendor, they acted as substitutes. The animals discriminated between poker chips having a food reward value and those having no such value. In a discrimination situation, the animals came to select one of two chips, one having twice the food-getting value of the other. The tokens effectively induced work in delayed-reward situa-tions, provided there was not too long a delay between insertion of the chip in a vendor and appearance of the food. Very effective was the situation in which the animals secured a token that they later exchanged for food. When work was done

for a given time and then rewarded in proportion to its amount, grapes and tokens were equally effective incentives. Tokens elicited competitive behavior comparable with that elicited by food. A token appropriate to a hunger or thirst need could be selected. Many similar observations are included in the study. (PsycINFO Database Record (c) 2012 APA, all rights reserved)

Zimmerman, E. H., Zimmerman, J., & Russell, C. D. (1969). Differential effects of token reinforcement on instruction-following behavior in retarded students instructed as a group. *Journal of Applied Behavior Analysis, 2,* 101–112.

This study addresses the problem of applying behavior modification techniques on a group basis to a class of retarded students with "attentional deficits." Seven boys aged 8 to 15 years old, characterized as showing severe "attentional" problems or disruptive behavior in their respective classrooms, participated daily for 30-minute sessions in a special class over a 1.5-month period. In each session, verbal instructions were given to the class as a whole. In control sessions, each appropriate instruction-following response by a child produced praise for that child. In experimental sessions, appropriate responses also produced tokens exchangeable for tangible reinforcers after the session. Token reinforcement differentially maintained instruction-following behavior in four children, while one responded appropriately to most instructions and a second improved continuously during the study. While the data suggest that the present approach can be successfully applied to the alteration of instruction-following behavior in retarded children, its major contribution may be that of providing objective quantitative information about such behavior.

Zimmerman, J., Stuckey, T. E., Garlick, B. J., & Miller, M. (1969). Effects of token reinforcement on productivity in multiple handicapped clients in a sheltered workshop. *Rehabilitation Literature, 30,* 34–41.

No abstract is available for this article.

Zirpoli, T. J. (2008). *Behavior management: Applications for teachers.* New Jersey: Prentice Hall.

Zlomke, K., & Zlomke, L. (2003). Token economy plus self-monitoring to reduce disruptive classroom behaviors. *Behavior Analyst Today, 4*(2), 177.

The current study examines the effectiveness of a combined token economy and self-monitoring package with a youth displaying a major mental illness and severe aggressive and persistent disruptive behaviors. The student received points for lower rates of aggressive/disruptive behavior and "bonus" points for accurately self-monitoring and recording his own behaviors. The results indicate that the addition of the self-monitoring component decreased the number of targeted behaviors beyond the substantial reduction of the token economy alone. In the reversal, there was a slight rise in the emission of problem behaviors, yet the frequency was still significantly below baseline. Implications for clinical applications and future research are discussed. (PsycINFO Database Record (c) 2014 APA, all rights reserved)

CREDITS

1986, http://psycnet.apa.org/psycinfo/1987-14003-001. Copyright © 2012 by American Psychological Association.

J. S. Birnbrauer, M. M. Wolf, J. D. Kidder, and Cecilia E. Tague, Abstract from: "Classroom Behavior of Retarded Pupils with Token Reinforcement," *Journal of Experimental Child Psychology*, vol. 2, issue 2. Copyright © 1965 by Elsevier B.V. Reprinted with permission.

Kurt A. Boniecki and Stacy Moore, Abstract from: "Breaking the Silence: Using a Token Economy to Reinforce Classroom Participation," *Teaching of Psychology*, vol. 30 no. 3. Copyright © 2003 by SAGE Publications.

PsycINFO Abstract for: Marcia Broden, R. Vance Hall, Ann Dunlap, and Robert Clark, "Effects of Teacher Attention and a Token Reinforcement System in a Junior High School Special Education Class," *Exceptional Children*, vol. 36, issue 5, Sage Publications, http://psycnet.apa.org/psycinfo/1970-21533-001. Copyright © 2012 by American Psychological Association.

Sam F. Broughton and Benjamin B. Lahey, Abstract from: "Direct and Collateral Effects of Positive Reinforcement, Response-Cost, and Mixed Contingencies for Academic Performance," *Journal of School Psychology*, vol. 16, no. 2. Copyright © 1978 by Elsevier B.V.

John D. Burchard and Francisco Barrera, Abstract from: "An Analysis of Timeout and Response Cost in a Programmed Environment," *Journal of Applied Behavior Analysis*, vol. 5, issue 3. Copyright © 1972 by John Wiley & Sons, Inc.

Amy Campbell and Cynthia M. Anderson, Abstract from: "Check-in/Check-out: A Systematic Evaluation and Component Analysis," *Journal of Applied Behavior Analysis*, vol. 44, issue 2. Copyright © 2011 by John Wiley & Sons, Inc.

R. G. Carey, M. D. Mosk, and K. B. Kranchuck, Abstract from: "Employing Overcorrection as a Cost Contingency in a Token Economy," *Behavior Research of Severe Developmental Disabilities*, vol. 2. Copyright © 1981 by Elsevier B.V.

Albert R. Cavalier, Ralph P. Ferretti, and Amelia E. Hodges, Abstract from: "Self-Management within a Classroom Token Economy for Students with Learning Disabilities," *Research in Developmental Disabilities*, vol. 18, issue 3. Copyright © 1997 by Elsevier B.V. Reprinted with permission.

PsycINFO Abstract for: David B. Center and Alan M. Wascom, "Transfer of Reinforcers: A Procedure for Enhancing Response Cost," *Educational and Psychological Research*, vol. 4, issue 1, University of Southern Mississippi, 1984, http://psycnet.apa.org/psycinfo/1985-10798-001. Copyright © by American Psychological Association.

Chiu-Wen Chen and Hsen-Hsing Ma, Abstract from: "Effects of Treatment on Disruptive Behaviors: A Quantitative Synthesis of Single-Subject Researches Using the PEM Approach," *Behavior Analyst Today*, vol. 8, no. 4. Copyright © 2007 by American Psychological Association.

Edward R. Christophersen, Caroline M. Arnold, Diane W. Hill, and H. Robert Quilitch, Abstract from: "The Home Point System: Token Reinforcement Procedures for Application by Parents of Children with

Behavior Problems," *Journal of Applied Behavior Analysis*, vol. 5, issue 4. Copyright © 1972 by John Wiley & Sons, Inc.

Marilyn Clark, Joe Lachowicz, and Montrose Wolf, Abstract from: "A Pilot Basic Education Program for School Dropouts Incorporating a Token Reinforcement System," *Behaviour Research and Therapy*, vol. 6, issue 2. Copyright © 1968 by Elsevier B.V.

Joseph E. Comaty, Michael Stasiob, and Claire Advokat, Abstract from: "Analysis of Outcome Variables of a Token Economy System in a State Psychiatric Hospital: A Program Evaluation," *Research in Developmental Disabilities*, vol. 22, issue 3. Copyright © 2001 by Elsevier B.V. Reprinted with permission.

Carole Conyers, Raymond Miltenberger, Amber Maki, Rebecca Barenz, Mandy Jurgens, Angela Sailer, Meredith Haugen, and Brandon Kopp, Abstract from: "A Comparison of Response Cost and Differential Reinforcement of Other Behavior to Reduce Disruptive Behavior in a Preschool Classroom," *Journal of Applied Behavior Analysis*, vol. 37, issue 3. Copyright © 2004 by John Wiley & Sons, Inc.

PsycINFO Abstract for: Patrick W. Corrigan, "Use of Token Economy with Seriously Mentally Ill Patients: Criticisms and Misconceptions," *Psychiatric Services*, vol. 46, issue 12, American Psychiatric Association, 1995, http://psycnet.apa.org/psycinfo/1996-31461-001. Copyright © 2012 by American Psychological Association.

Sherwin B. Cotler, Gary Applegate, Larry W. King, and Stan Kristal, Abstract from: "Establishing a Token Economy Program in a State Hospital Classroom: A Lesson in Training Student and Teacher," *Behavior Therapy*, vol. 3, issue 2. Copyright © 1972 by Elsevier B.V. Reprinted with permission.

A. J. Dalton, C. A. Rubino, and M. W. Hislop, Abstract from: "Some Effects of Token Rewards on School Achievement of Children with Down's Syndrome," *Journal of Applied Behavior Analysis*, vol. 6, issue 2. Copyright © 1973 by John Wiley & Sons, Inc.

Faith B. Dickerson, Wendy N. Tenhulab, and Lisa D. Green-Paden, Abstract from: "The Token Economy for Schizophrenia: Review of the Literature and Recommendations for Future Research," *Schizophrenia Research*, vol. 75, issues 2-3. Copyright © 2005 by Elsevier B.V.

Peter B. Everett, Scott C. Hayward, and Andrew W. Meyers, Abstract from: "The Effects of a Token Reinforcement Procedure on Bus Ridership," *Journal of Applied Behavior Analysis*, vol. 7, issue 1. Copyright © 1974 by John Wiley & Sons, Inc.

Holly A. Filcheck and Cheryl B. McNeil, Abstract from: "The Use of Token Economies in Preschool Classrooms: Practical and Philosophical Concerns," *Journal of Early and Intensive Behavior Intervention*, vol. 1, no. 1. Copyright © 2004 by American Psychological Association.

Holly A. Filcheck, Cheryl B. McNeil, Laurie A. Greco, and Rebecca S. Bernard, Abstract from: "Using a Whole-Class Token Economy and Coaching of Teacher Skills in a Preschool Classroom to Manage Disruptive Behavior," *Psychology in the Schools*, vol. 41, issue 3. Copyright © 2004 by John Wiley & Sons, Inc.

ERIC Institute of Education Sciences Abstract for: Bill W. Hillman, "The Effect of Knowledge of Results and Token Reinforcement on the Arithmetic Achievement of Elementary School Children," *The Arithmetic Teacher*, vol. 17, issue 9, National Council of Teachers of Mathematics, 1970, http://eric. ed.gov/?id=EJ031275. Published by U.S. Department of Education.

Michael M. Holt, Tom R. Hobbs, and Ron Hankins, Abstract from: "The Fffects of Token Reinforcement on Delinquents' Classroom Behavior," *Psychology in the Schools*, vol. 13, issue 3. Copyright © 1976 by John Wiley & Sons, Inc.

PsycINFO Abstract for: James G. Hunt and Joseph Zimmerman, "Stimulating Productivity in a Simulated Sheltered Workshop Setting," *American Journal of Mental Deficiency, vol. 74, issue 1, American Association on Intellectual Developmental Disabilities*, 1969, http://psycnet.apa.org/index.cfm?fa=search.displayRec ord&UID=1969-17545-001. Copyright © 2012 by American Psychological Association.

Roger J. Ingham and Gavin Andrews, Abstract from: "An Analysis of a Token Economy in Stuttering Therapy," *Journal of Applied Behavior Analysis,* vol. 6, issue 2. Copyright © 1973 by John Wiley & Sons, Inc.

ERIC Institute of Education Sciences Abstract for: J. A. Inkster and T. F. McLaughlin, "Token Reinforcement: Effects for Reducing Tardiness with a Socially Disadvantaged Adolescent Student," *B.C. Journal of Special Education*, vol. 17, no. 2, The University of British Columbia, 1992, http://eric.ed.gov/?id=EJ477595. Published by U.S. Department of Education.

Brian A. Iwata and Jon S. Bailey, Abstract from: "Reward Versus Cost Token Systems: An Analysis of the Effects on Students and Teacher," *Journal of Applied Behavior Analysis*, vol. 7, issue 4. Copyright © 1974 by John Wiley & Sons, Inc.

Alan E. Kazdin, Abstract from: "Toward a Client Administered Token Reinforcement Program," *Education and Training of the Mentally Retarded*, vol. 6, no. 2. Copyright © 1971 by Council for Exceptional Children.

Alan E. Kazdin, Abstract from: "The Effect of Response Cost in Suppressing Behavior in a Pre-Psychotic Retardate," *Journal of Behavior Therapy and Experimental Psychiatry*, vol. 2, issue 2. Copyright © 1971 by Elsevier B.V.

Alan E. Kazdin, Abstract from: "Response Cost: The Removal of Conditioned Reinforcers for Therapeutic Change," *Behavior Therapy*, vol. 3, issue 4. Copyright © 1972 by Elsevier B.V. Reprinted with permission.

Alan E. Kazdin, Abstract from: "The Effect of Vicarious Reinforcement on Attentive Behavior in the Classroom," *Journal of Applied Behavior Analysis*, vol. 6, issue 1. Copyright © 1973 by John Wiley & Sons, Inc.

Alan E. Kazdin, Abstract from: "The Token Economy: A Decade Later," *Journal of Applied Behavior Analysis*, vol. 15, issue 3. Copyright © 1982 by John Wiley & Sons, Inc.

Alan E. Kazdin and Richard R. Bootzin, Abstract from: "The Token Economy: An Evaluative Review," *Journal of Applied Behavior Analysis*, vol. 5, issue 3. Copyright © 1972 by John Wiley & Sons, Inc.

Applied Behavior Analysis, vol. 32, issue 3, John Wiley & Sons, Inc., 1999, http://eric.ed.gov/?id=EJ594942. Published by U.S. Department of Education.

ERIC Institute of Education Sciences Abstract for: Kara E. McGoey and George J. DuPaul, "Token Reinforcement and Response Cost Procedures: Reducing the Disruptive Behavior of Preschool Children with Attention-Deficit/Hyperactivity Disorder," *School Psychology Quarterly*, vol. 15, no. 3, American Psychological Association, 2000, http://eric.ed.gov/?id=EJ614400. Published by U.S. Department of Education.

PsycINFO Abstract for: Hugh S. Mckenzie, M. Clark, M. M. Wolf, R. Kothera, and C. Benson, "Behavior Modification of Children with Learning Disabilities Using Grades as Tokens and Allowances as Back Up Reinforcers," *Exceptional Children*, vol. 34, issue 10, 1968, http://psycnet.apa.org/psycinfo/1969-11835-001. Copyright © 2013 by American Psychological Association.

PsycINFO Abstract for: T. F. McLaughlin, "The Applicability of Token Reinforcement Systems in Public School Systems," *Psychology in the Schools*, vol. 12, issue 1, John Wiley & Sons, Inc., 1975, http://psycnet.apa.org/psycinfo/1975-30527-001. Copyright © 2012 by American Psychological Association.

Thomas F. McLaughlin and John Malaby, Abstract from: "Intrinsic Reinforcers in a Classroom Token Economy," *Journal of Applied Behavior Analysis*, vol. 5, issue 3. Copyright © 1972 by John Wiley & Sons, Inc.

L. Keith Miller and Richard Schneider, Abstract from: "The Use of a Token System in Project Head Start," *Journal of Applied Behavior Analysis*, vol. 3, issue 3. Copyright © 1970 by John Wiley & Sons, Inc.

PsycINFO Abstract for: James K. Music and Robert E. Luckey, "Program Profiles: A Token Economy for Moderately and Severely Retarded," *Mental Retardation*, vol. 8, issue 1, American Association on Intellectual Developmental Disabilities, 1970, http://psycnet.apa.org/psycinfo/1972-11483-001. Copyright © 1970 by American Psychological Association.

ERIC Institute of Education Sciences Abstract for: Colleen C. Naughton and T. F. McLaughlin, "The Use of a Token Economy System for Students with Behaviour Disorders," *B.C. Journal of Special Education*, vol. 19, no. 2-3, The University of British Columbia, 1995, http://eric.ed.gov/?id=EJ519926. Published by U.S. Department of Education.

K. Daniel O'Leary and Wesley C. Becker, Abstract from: "Behavior Modification of an Adjustment Class: A Token Reinforcement Program," *Exceptional Children*, vol. 33, issue 9. Copyright © 1967 by SAGE Publications.

PsycINFO Abstract for: K. Daniel O'Leary and Ronald Drabman, "Token Reinforcement Programs in the Classroom: A Review," *Psychological Bulletin*, vol. 75, issue 6, American Pscyhological Association, 1971, http://psycnet.apa.org/psycinfo/1972-01793-001. Copyright © 2012 by American Psychological Association.

Elery L. Phillips, Abstract from: "Achievement Place: Token Reinforcement Procedures in a Home-Style Rehabilitation Setting for "Pre-Delinquent' Boys," *Journal of Applied Behavior Analysis*, vol. 1, issue 3. Copyright © 1968 by John Wiley & Sons, Inc.

Terrence Piper, Abstract from: "A Token Reinforcement Procedure in a Third Grade Inner City Classroom," *Education*, vol. 92, issue 3. Copyright © 1972 by Project Innovation, Inc.

ERIC Institute of Education Sciences Abstract for: Mark D. Rapport, Al Murphy, and Jon S. Bailey, "The Effects of a Response Cost Treatment Tactic on Hyperactive Children," *Journal of School Psychology*, vol. 18, issue 2, Elsevier B.V., 1980, http://eric.ed.gov/?id=EJ227447. Published by U.S. Department of Education.

David Reitman, Molly A. Murphy, Stephen D. A. Hupp, and Patrick M. O'Callaghan, Abstract from: "Behavior Change and Perceptions of Change: Evaluating the Effectiveness of a Token Economy," *Child & Family Behavior Therapy*, vol. 26, issue 2. Copyright © 2004 by Taylor & Francis Group. Available at: http://www.tandfonline.com.

V. M. J. Ringer, Abstract from: "The Use of a 'Token Helper' in the Management of Classroom Behavior Problems and in Teacher Training," *Journal of Applied Behavior Analysis*, vol. 6, issue 4. Copyright © 1973 by John Wiley & Sons, Inc.

Abstract from: Carl L. Roberts and Robert M. Perry, "A Total Token Economy," *Mental Retardation*, vol. 8, issue 1, American Association on Intellectual Developmental Disabilities, 1970, http://psycnet.apa.org/psycinfo/1972-11489-001. Copyright © 2015 by American Psychological Association.

Robert S. Ruskin and Roger F. Maley, Abstract from: "Item Preference in a Token Economy Ward Store," *Journal of Applied Behavior Analysis*, vol. 5, issue 3. Copyright © 1972 by John Wiley & Sons, Inc.

Spencer J. Salend and Elizabeth Marie Allen, Abstract from: "Comparative Effects of Externally Managed and Self-Managed Response-Cost Systems on Inappropriate Classroom Behavior," *Journal of School Psychology*, vol. 23, issue 1. Copyright © 1985 by Elsevier B.V.

ERIC Institute of Education Sciences Abstract for: Spencer J. Salend, Linda Tintle, and Hillary Balber, "Effects of a Student-Managed Response-Cost System on the Behavior of Two Mainstreamed Students," *Elementary School Journal*, vol. 89, no. 1, University of Chicago Press, 1988, http://eric.ed.gov/?id=EJ377922. Published by U.S. Department of Education.

National Association of School Psychologists Abstract for: Howard E. Sattler and Karen S. Swoope, "Token Systems: A Procedural Guide," http://www.nasponline.org/publications/spr/abstract.aspx?ID=11. Copyright © by National Association of School Psychologists.

Gerald M. Siegel, Joanne Lenske, and Patricia Broen, Abstract from: "Suppression of Normal Speech Influencies Through Response Cost," *Journal of Applied Behavior Analysis*, vol. 2, issue 4. Copyright © 1969 by John Wiley & Sons, Inc.

Sandeep K. Sran and John C. Borrero, Abstract from: "Assessing the Value of Choice in a Token System," *Journal of Applied Behavior Analysis*, vol. 43, issue 3. Copyright © 2010 by John Wiley & Sons, Inc.

Arthur W. Staats, Karl A. Minke, and Priscilla Butts, Abstract from: "A Token-Reinforcement Remedial Reading Program Administered by Black Therapy-Technicians to Problem Black Children," *Behavior Therapy*, vol. 1, issue 3. Copyright © 1970 by Elsevier B.V. Reprinted with permission.

Arthur W. Staats, Carolyn K. Staats, Richard E. Schutz, and Montrose Wolf, Abstract from: "The Conditioning of Textual Responses Using 'Extrinsic' Reinforcers," *Journal of the Experimental Analysis of Behavior*, vol. 5, issue 1. Copyright © 1962 by John Wiley & Sons, Inc.

Maureen A. Sullivan and Susan G. O'Leary, Abstract from: "Maintenance Following Reward and Cost Token Programs," *Behavior Therapy*, vol. 21, issue 1. Copyright © 1990 by Elsevier B.V.

James C. Swain and T. F. McLaughlin, Abstract from: "The Effects of Bonus Contingencies in a Classwide Token Program on Math Accuracy with Middle-School Students with Behavioral Disorders," *Behavioral Interventions*, vol. 13, issue 1. Copyright © 1998 by John Wiley & Sons, Inc.

Naomi B. Swiezy, Johnny L. Matson, and Peggy Box, Abstract from: "The Good Behavior Game: A Token Reinforcement System for Preschoolers," *Child & Family Behavior Therapy*, vol. 14, issue 3. Copyright © 1993 by Taylor & Francis Group.

Marla Truchlicka, T. F. McLaughlin, and James C. Swain, Abstract from: "Effects of Token Reinforcement and Response Cost on the Accuracy of Spelling Performance with Middle-School Special Education Students with Behavior Disorders," *Behavioral Interventions,* vol. 13, issue 1. Copyright © 1998 by John Wiley & Sons, Inc.

Vernon O. Tyler, Jr., Abstract from: "Application of Operant Token Reinforcement to Academic Performance of an Institutionalized Delinquent," *Psychological Reports*, vol. 21. Copyright © 1967 by Ammons Scientific, Ltd.

PsycINFO Abstract for: Vernon O. Tyler, Jr. and G. Duane Brown, "Token Reinforcement of Academic Performance with Institutionalized Delinquent Boys," *Journal of Educational Psychology*, vol. 59, issue 3, American Psychological Association, 1968, http://psycnet.apa.org/psycinfo/1968-12409-001. Copyright © 2012 by American Psychological Association.

Rudolph F. Wagner and Barbara P. Guyer, Excerpt from: "Maintenance of Discipline Through Increasing Children's Span of Attending by Means of a Token Economy," *Psychology in the Schools*, vol. 8, issue 3. Copyright © 1971 by John Wiley & Sons, Inc.

Harold Weiner, Abstract from: "Some Effects of Response Cost upon Human Operant Behavior," *Journal of the Experimental Analysis of Behavior*, vol. 5, issue 2. Copyright © 1962 by John Wiley & Sons, Inc.

Richard A. Winett, C. Steven Richards, Leonard Krasner, and Miriam Krasner, Excerpt from: "Child-Monitored Token Reading Program," *Psychology in the Schools*, vol. 8, issue 3. Copyright © 1971 by John Wiley & Sons, Inc.

R.C. Winkler, Abstract from: "The Relevance of Economic Theory and Technology to Token Reinforcement Systems," *Behaviour Research and Therapy*, vol. 9, issue 2. Copyright © 1971 by Elsevier B.V.

References

The following are references used in the text but not listed in the previous Chapter 12, "Literature."

Deibert, A. S., & Harmon, A. (1970). *New Tools for Changing Behavior*. Champaign, IL: Research Press.

Dewey, J. (1938). *Experience and Education*. West Lafayette, IN: Kappa Delta Pi.

Filcheck, H. A., McNeil, C. B., Greco, L. A., & Bernard, R. S. (2004). Using a whole-class token economy and coaching of teacher skills in a preschool classroom to manage disruptive behavior. *Psychology in the Schools, 41*, 351–361. doi:10.1002/pits.10168

Gall, M., Gall, J. S., & Borg, W. (2006). *Educational Research: An introduction* (8th ed.) Boston: Pearson, Allyn & Bacon.

Homme, L. (1969). *How to Use Contingency Contracting in the Classroom*. Champaign, IL: Research Press.

Kavale, K. (2001). Meta-analysis: A primer. *Exceptionality, 9*, 177–183. doi:10.1207/S15327035EX0904-2

Klimas, A., & McLaughlin, T. F. (2007). The effects of a token economy system to improve social and academic behavior with a rural primary-aged child with disabilities. *International Journal of Special Education, 22*(3).

Kuypers, D. S., Becker, W. C., & O'Leary, K. D. (1968). How to make a token system fail. *Exceptional Children, 35(2)*, 101–109.

Lindsley, O. (1963). *Free-operant Conditioning and Psychotherapy: Current Psychiatric Therapies.* New York: Grune & Stratton.

Lipsey, M. S., & Wilson, D. (2001). *Practical Meta-analysis.* Applied Social Research Methods Series (vol. 49). Thousand Oaks, CA: Sage Publications.

Payne, J., Polloway, E., Kauffman, J. M., & Scranton, T. (1975). *Living in the Classroom: The Currency-Based Token Economy.* New York: Human Sciences Press.

Peddiwell, J. (1939). *The Saber-Tooth Curriculum.* New York: McGraw-Hill.

Premack, D. (1959). Toward Empirical Behavior Laws: Positive Reinforcement. *Psychological Review, 66*, 219–233.

Premack, D. (1965). Reinforcement Theory. In D. Levine (Ed.), *Nebraska Symposium on Motivation.* Lincoln: University of Nebraska Press.

Salend, S., & Lamb, E. (1986). Effectiveness of a group-managed interdependent contingency system. *Learning Disability Quarterly, 9*, 268–273.

Salend, S. J., Tintle, L., and Balber, H. (1988). Effects of a student-managed response cost system on the behavior of two mainstreamed students. *Elementary School Journal, 89*(1), 89–97.

Skinner, B. (1953). *Science and Human Behavior.* New York: Macmillan.

Soares, D. (2011). *Effect Size and Moderators of Effects for Token Economy Interventions.* (Unpublished doctoral dissertation). Texas A&M University, College Station, TX.

Stainback, W., Payne, J., Stainback, S., & Payne, R. (1973). *Establishing a Token Economy in the Classroom.* Columbus, OH: Charles E. Merrill.

Sran, S. K., & Borrero, J. C. (2010). Assessing the value of choice in a token system. *Journal of Applied Behavior Analysis, 43*, 553–557.

Stevens, C., Siddener, T., Reeve, S., & Siddener, D. W. (2011). Effects of behavior-specific and general praise on acquisition of tacts in children with pervasive developmental disorders. *Research in Autism Spectrum Disorders, 5*, 666–669. doi:10.1016/j.read.2010.08.003

Truchlicka, M., McLaughlin, T. F., & Swain, J. C. (1998). Effects of token reinforcement and response cost on the accuracy of spelling performance with middle-school special education students with behavior disorders. *Behavioral Interventions, 13*, 1–10. doi:10.1002-(SICI)1099-078X(199802)13:1<1::AID-BINI>3.0CO;2-Z

Appendix

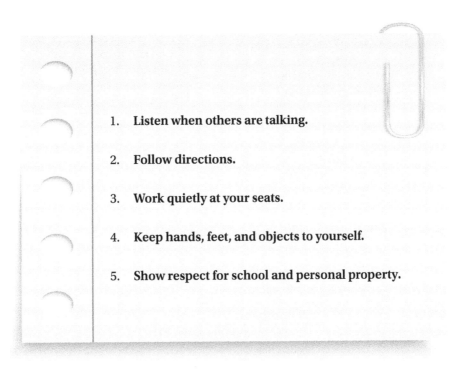

Appendix Figure 1. Visual Chart of Expected Behavior. Copyright © Depositphotos/human_306.

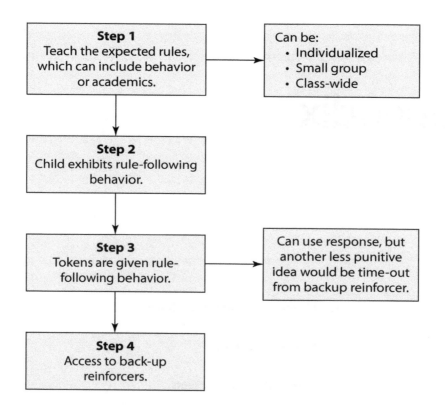

Appendix figure 2. Simple Steps for a Token Economy

Appendix Table 1. No-Cost Backup Reinforcers

Reinforcer	Example
Special jobs in the class	A student wants to be an office assistant or assist with the custodians.
Computer time	Student wants to play an academic game for 15 minutes.
Academic extra assistance	Free answer on one test item, homework pass, late assignment pass (limited to a few days within the due date).
Special chair or work location	Student wants to sit in the teacher's rolling chair for the day or student can sit in a beanbag to do work.
Positive note home or phone call	Additional positive note home so that child can receive or do something special.
Buddy time	Work with a buddy for an assignment.
Choose your desk	Get to pick where you want to sit in the classroom. I generally gave three choices so that I could keep students away from negative situations.

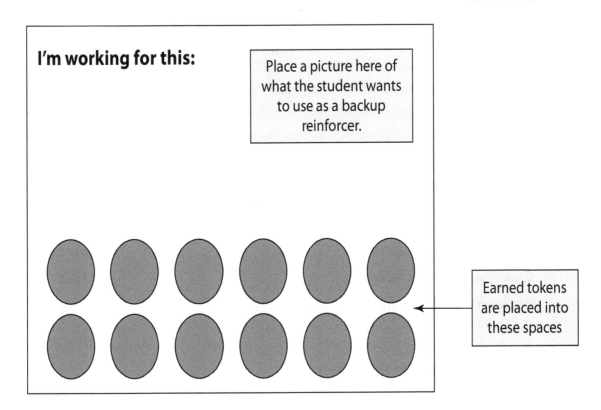

I'm working for this:

Place a picture here of what the student wants to use as a backup reinforcer.

Earned tokens are placed into these spaces

Appendix figure 3. Sample Token Card.

How will you spend your tokens?

Reinforcer	Price
Mystery box A	20
Mystery box B	30
15 minutes on computer	35
Lunch with a friend	45
Use teacher's chair for a day	60

Appendix figure 4. Sample Reward Menu.

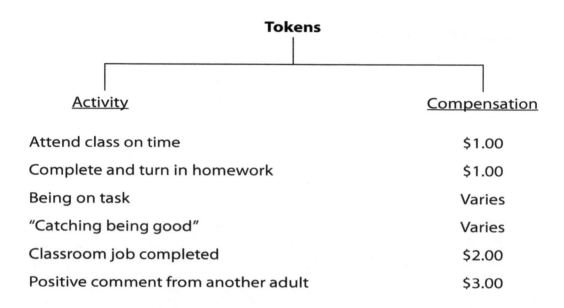

Tokens

Activity	Compensation
Attend class on time	$1.00
Complete and turn in homework	$1.00
Being on task	Varies
"Catching being good"	Varies
Classroom job completed	$2.00
Positive comment from another adult	$3.00

Appendix Figure 5. Token Menu Sample.

(Child's name)'s School Behavior Chart

	Kept hands to self	Followed directions	Behaved at lunch	Teacher comments	Parent's signature
Monday					
Tuesday					
Wednesday					
Thursday					
Friday					

Week of: _____

Appendix Figure 6. Student Behavior Chart.

Example

Appendix Fgure 7. Marble Jar. Copyright © Depositphotos/kozzi2.

Printed in Australia
AUHW021428260821
351033AU00016B/34